CW00547682

# *Yes! No! But Wait...!*

THE ONE THING YOU NEED TO KNOW TO WRITE A NOVEL

TIM LOTT

SWIFT PRESS

First published in Great Britain by Swift Press 2023

10 9 8 7 6 5 4 3 2 1



Typeset by Tetragon, London
Printed in England by CPI Group (UK) Ltd, Croydon, CRO 4YY

A CIP catalogue record for this book is available from the British Library

ISBN: 9781800752214
eISBN: 9781800752221

Printed and bound in the UK on FSC® certified paper in line with our continuing commitment to ethical business practices, sustainability and the environment.
**For further information see faber.co.uk/environmental-policy**

To my mentors and friends, Robert McKee, John Yorke and Will Storr, without whom I would have remained lost in the woods. Also David Mamet and Joseph Campbell, who have been inspirations for me in both life and writing.

What do we wish for in the perfect game?

Do we wish for Our Team to take the field and thrash the opposition from the First Moment, rolling up a walkover score at the final gun?

No. We wish for a closely fought match that contains many satisfying reversals, but which can be seen, retroactively, to have always tended toward a satisfying and inevitable conclusion.

We wish, in effect, for a three-act structure... In which... each act of the game recapitulates the game (following the paradigm: 'Yes! No! But wait...!').

DAVID MAMET,
*Three Uses of the Knife: On the Nature and Purpose of Drama* (1998)

# CONTENTS

# LIST OF ILLUSTRATIONS

# PREFACE

## *The One Thing You Need to Know*

When I originally had the idea for *Yes! No! But Wait…!* I wanted it to be the most straightforward and accessible book on writing a work of fiction ever published.

I was also determined to make it the most honest.

That immediately presented me with a problem.

Because then I had no choice but to confess that the book I wanted to write wouldn't teach anyone how to write a novel.

No one can do that.

Not even people who write novels know how to write novels.

That's why promising young novelists often run out of steam after one or two books. And why very good novelists sometimes write mediocre or bad novels.

I know – because I've spent the last fifteen years trying to teach people how to write fiction (while actually writing novels, ten at the last count, in the time left in between).

I've read and critiqued hundreds of manuscripts by would-be authors.

The results have all pointed towards the same conclusion.

Which is that writing a novel – at least, a good novel – is hard.

Really hard.

(Although it should be borne in mind that there is a considerable market for bad novels.)

You can read all the 'How To' books you like, go on all the courses you want, but if you don't have a respectable quantity of talent, a prodigious amount of willpower, great reserves of self-discipline and the ability to sit alone in a room for very long periods, you are unlikely to go the full stretch.

All the same – I hope this is the most useful book on the subject you will ever read.

Because it calls out the dream factory of the highly profitable and ever-hungry creative-writing industry – which stretches from the universities, to the halls of publishing and literary agencies, and to innumerable mentoring services and websites. Then there are countless video courses, lectures and evening classes in far-flung town halls.

Many of these individual sites and courses are perfectly good, sometimes excellent, at what they do. I wouldn't teach for *Guardian* Masterclasses if I didn't believe it to be an outstanding example of what the teaching industry can achieve. Or have spent my years with the Faber Academy.

The trouble is, *taken all together*, they muddy the water rather than purify it.

In a way that is not quite duplicitous, but definitely questionable.

The creative-writing industry, as a whole, sprawls like a cuddly, beckoning parasite over would-be writers everywhere in the Anglosphere and beyond.

Without ever stating the case baldly, it tells all the hopefuls out there, dreaming of being the new J. K. Rowling or Jonathan Franzen or Bernardine Evaristo, that anyone can write a novel – and then pockets their money for the privilege of being sold a glittering but usually unrealisable chimera.

These courses are often a great source of fun and camaraderie. They certainly offer a huge range of information and advice.

Far *too* much – in my view.

Because there is only *one thing* you really need to know.

One thing that towers over the rest of the creative-writing landscape like a behemoth – but which is all too often obscured, at least partially, by the sheer volume of choice and possibility offered by colleges, universities and private organisations.

What is that one thing?

ooooo

Storytelling is a mystery.

It's *such* a mystery that Hollywood can spend millions of dollars putting together a story on-screen, using the best writers, script editors, directors and producers in the world.

They know all the books on storytelling backwards and have probably written a few themselves.

Then they still manage to come up with something that stinks to the heavens.

Because all the craft in the world doesn't get you a hit movie.

Or hit novel.

Or a hit play.

Then again, neither does pure talent.

From time to time, an unusually gifted writer emerges capable of producing a publishable, or even great, novel without having to think much about *how* it is being done.

Some writers have an almost uncanny feel for structure and character, and for them, things just fall into place automatically.

Those chosen few just... *do it.*

It may be inborn talent, or it may be as a result of learning the craft by osmosis, that is, via a lifelong habit (which all writers share) of compulsively consuming stories on the page and screen. This leaves an unconscious residue that some fortunate people can just draw on without having to think much about it.

So – if you think you can write a novel without any help, then there is nothing to stop you.

Put this book back on the shelf, walk away and get writing.

After all, if storytelling is an impenetrable mystery, why bother trying to learn it?

That's why this book doesn't promise you it can teach you to write a good novel. Or any kind of novel at all.

But it *does* tell you everything that it is helpful to know before you start to try – after which, if truth be told, you are on your own.

It is not a handbook to be systematically referred to.

As one of my storytelling heroes, Robert McKee, remarked during one of his brilliant lectures, 'You only think of this stuff when your writing is NOT WORKING.'

It's a fallback position – something to turn to when you're stuck, a roughly drawn map when you're lost – and a useful editing tool.

It's NOT a blueprint for 'how to write a story'.

I rarely start a novel with the ideas in this book laid out in front of me consciously.

But when I am stuck, those ideas drift to the surface and lend me help.

Or, when I am editing my novels, they remind me of the ideal shape of a piece of fiction, which I am at liberty to conform to or ignore.

Many highly salaried tutors and financially shrewd website owners tell you (or, more often, imply) that if you put craft at the forefront of your mind – bingo, you will be able to write a novel, assuming you study assiduously enough. Hence the popularity of three- or even four-year novel-writing courses – a case of overkill if ever there was one.

This book, on the other hand, doesn't waste tens of thousands of words telling you about everything you *can't* learn.

Because most fiction skills can't be taught.

Or rather, they can be taught – and they are, endlessly – but they can rarely be learned.

Most skills are a matter of instinct, practice, deep reading, habit, luck, insight, imagination and willpower.

They are lodged deep in the unconscious mind. Or they emerge from long practice and emerge as the fruit of many failed attempts.

Such qualities cannot be purchased at any price.

ooooo

A story is organic – not rational or analytical – in that everything in a story is connected to everything else.

You *grow* a story.

A novel is not a job to be done – it is an exploration to be undertaken.

Having said that, every art has its craft, and storytelling is no exception.

As well as artists, writers are *wordsmiths* – like blacksmiths or silversmiths.

That is to say, there is a 'making' part to this growing of stories.

And there *are* techniques to help you do that – whether you are a thriller writer, a literary writer, a dramatist or a screenwriter.

This is a book about those techniques – the *craft* of storytelling, the ghostly, bare scaffolding on which a writer can hang the verdant products of their imagination.

Above all, there is one thing that needs to be learned before you get started trying to write your novel *on your own* (which is how all writers have always worked since writing began).

And that thing *is* teachable – if you work hard to understand it, ingest it and make it your servant (no writer should ever have a master).

That one thing is the sole subject of this book.

The One Thing has *two* aspects – *plot* and *character*.

I describe them, quite correctly, as 'One Thing' because they are two sides of the same coin, intermingled strands of the same double helix.

They are unified by the principle of *change*. Both plot and character will be in a state of continual change throughout the story.

Change one and you change the other.

Plot and character, tied together by change, are the essential ingredients for any screenplay, novel, short story, drama or TV series.

Master them and you have mastered the foundations of storytelling.

Then you can start to build.

# I

# *Plot (Part One)*

## INTRODUCTION TO PLOT:
## *What is a plot anyway?*

Plot has long been unfashionable among certain sectors of the literary elite.

The screenwriting guru Robert McKee notes the persistence of this anti-plot trend in his book *Story* (1997).

'Over the last 25 years,' he notes,

> the method of teaching creative writing in American universities has shifted from the intrinsic to the extrinsic. Trends in literary theory have drawn professors away from the deep sources of story toward language, codes, text – *story seen from the outside*. As a result, with some notable exceptions, the current generation of writers has been undereducated in the prime principles of story. [Chapter 1: 'The Story Problem']

Many writers themselves seem to cheerfully sign up to the war on plot.

'Well, fuck the plot! That is for precocious schoolboys. What matters is the imaginative truth,' said Edna O'Brien.

'Plots really matter only in thrillers,' declared Martin Amis.

'As far as I'm concerned, character is everything. I never did see why I have to throw in a plot too' – is the view of Anne Tyler.

It's not even a modern point of view.

'I have never troubled myself much about the construction of plots,' said Anthony Trollope (1815–82).

However, to me – despite the fact that I admire all of the above writers – such statements seem to be partly a form of aesthetic bravado and partly a defensive strategy peddled by writers who struggle with plot (which is practically every writer I know).

Try telling any great screenwriter, like David Chase (of *Sopranos* fame) or Jimmy McGovern or Russell T. Davies or Sally Wainwright, that plot is for 'precocious schoolboys' and you are likely – with respect to O'Brien, Amis, Tyler and Trollope – to be met with either extreme scepticism or, more likely, outright incredulity.

As Richard Skinner, head of the Faber Academy, puts it in his book *Fiction Writing* (2009):

> Somehow fiction that is plot-driven has over the years become synonymous with poorer quality, cheapness,

> contempt even. Malign it if you will, but ignore it at your peril, for plot is the 'thrust' of a narrative and its *genetic code* [my italics]. Without it, a narrative seems lifeless, without energy, inert. A narrative that is weakly plotted feels as though it will never get started and then you think it is never going to end.

This part of the genetic code, however, can be frustratingly elusive.

This is why, as a writing teacher, I can't help but notice that the primary problem that plagues an overwhelming number of my clients is usually the same one.

This problem is articulated perfectly by one of the greatest storytellers of the twentieth century, Patricia Highsmith, in *Plotting and Writing Suspense Fiction* (1966):

> The beginning writer's most frequent snag may take the form of the question, 'What happens next?' This is a terrifying question, which can leave the writer shaking with stage fright.

ooooo

*What happens next?*

It's certainly the question that scares me most as a novelist.

The problem with this problem is that I don't really have a solution.

I can make suggestions, but it's your book, and you have to decide what happens next.

It has to arise from your own imagination and be delivered in your own unique voice.

However, there are elements of the craft of storytelling that can assist you in deciding what happens next.

They are not rules or principles.

They are simply clues.

Before we get on to what some of the clues are, it's first worth asking two questions.

The first question is: 'What is a plot anyway?'

The second question is: 'Is the plot in a story the same as what happens in life?'

The answer to the second question is the simpler.

It's 'no'.

Plot isn't the same as life.

It couldn't be more different from life, in fact.

True – in life, stuff happens, just as stuff happens in a novel.

However, I don't know about your life, but most of my life is routine – not to say meaningless, chaotic and, as often as not, boring.

I scrub my teeth. I meet a friend. I watch TV. I cut my nails. I go shopping. I go to sleep. I wake up. I eat. I breathe. I read my credit card bill. I panic. I pick my nose. I water the plants. I stub my toe. I argue with my partner.

And so on.

In other words, like history, it's just one damn thing after another.

There's no particular order to it, other than that imposed by necessity, or chance, or the pursuit of desires or the avoidance of pain.

A plot is different.

George Saunders, in his book on writing, *A Swim in a Pond in the Rain* (2021), writes:

> The story is faster than real life, more compressed and exaggerated. A place where something new always has to be happening, something relevant to that which has already happened. ['A Page at a Time: Thoughts on "In the Cart"']

Alfred Hitchcock said of film plots that they were 'life with the boring bits taken out'.

But Hitchcock's definition is a very partial one.

It's not enough to take the boring bits out.

Because it will still be boring.

A plot also has to be meaningful.

That is, it will possess a particular architecture, designed consciously by the author to express something that author wants to communicate to the reader.

It is governed not (like life) by randomness, but by causality and theme.

It has a discernible beginning, middle and end (yes, in that order).

It is, as Aristotle wrote, 'the organisation of events'.

Plots have a *shape*.

And, remarkable though it may seem – in classic storytelling at least – they all have roughly the same shape.

We will come to the fascinating outlines of that universal shape later in this book.

For now, let's address the first, more penetrating, question.

What is a plot anyway?

## WHAT HOLDS A PLOT TOGETHER?: *Towards unity*

John Yorke, in *Into the Woods* (2013):

> A story is like a magnet dragged through randomness, pulling the chaos of things into some kind of shape and – if we're very lucky – some kind of sense. Every tale is an attempt to lasso a terrifying reality, tame it and bring it to heel. [Chapter 22: 'Why?']

Jean Rhys:

> To give life shape – is what a writer does.

Without *unity*, stories are just like life – a chaotic salad of events and happenings that have no shape or meaning.

For any novelist – or dramatist, or screenwriter – a story has to be transmuted into a coherent and unified *plot*.

How is this to be achieved?

By means of *theme*, *causality* and *purposefulness*.

ooooo

The *theme* of a story is one thing that might be said to hold a narrative together.

In this instance, events are arranged in order to demonstrate a point that the writer wants to make or to communicate, an idea they care about enough to spend years trying to express that idea at book length.

That idea, which will usually be too complex to be expressed directly, will be demonstrated not in words as such, but through a sequence of actions.

Action, not words, is the grammar of storytelling.

As one author once remarked about novel writing, 'Work out what you want to say, then spend the book not saying it.'

As McKee pointed out in a lecture, story is the '*dramatisation of truth*... the living expression and proof of a controlling idea *without explanation*'.

A 'controlling idea' is the same as a *theme*.

You don't have a character saying, 'Well, that proves it! Crime doesn't pay,' at the end of a detective story.

Or the heroine stating, 'Well, that proves it! True love conquers all,' at the end of a romance.

The action explains the meaning.

ooooo

When I worked as a screenwriter – I penned maybe a dozen commissioned screenplays in all – I spent a great deal of time in meetings with producers, directors and script editors, all of whom scratched their heads and worried away at the same question.

'What is this story really *about*?'

Once we'd solved that question, everything else began to fall into place.

Because finding the solution meant that we had discovered the *theme*.

The central idea binding the plot of *King Lear* together is that spiritual pride leads to a downfall (a common theme in classic stories).

*Lear* is about a very great deal more than this. Many volumes have been written about the nuances of that remarkable play. But at its heart, it is the depiction of a man who has let his great power go to his head so that he has become spiritually blind and emotionally stunted.

(His putative ally, the Earl of Gloucester, becomes *physically* blind – partly as a result of a similar mix of pride and naivety. Both the main plot and the subplot reinforce the theme.)

By the end of the play, Lear can 'see' again.

But unfortunately, it's too late.

Gloucester's blindness leads him to 'see'.

Also too late.

*C'est la vie.*

(The bemused, compassionate shrug is, as far as I am concerned, the most convincing of all story endings.)

So – *theme* is one clue to help you with the puzzle of what might come next in your story.

How?

You might ask yourself, 'What scene or event will contribute to developing this theme?'

And if you are lucky, you will get an answer – if you think and imagine hard enough, and experiment with sufficient tenacity.

There is a difficulty with this principle though (there's a difficulty with *everything* when it comes to writing).

Many writers don't know what their theme *is* until they are halfway through the book – since many writers simply make it up as they go along and hope for the best. That's certainly my 'technique', otherwise known as 'seatofpantsery'.

Some writers *finish* a book still having no idea what the theme is. They just write the book as it comes to them, then serve it up and hope for the best.

I once did an interview for students at the University of East Anglia, after I'd written maybe half a dozen novels, and the interviewer, Russell Celyn Jones, said this to me:

'All your books are about loss – aren't they?'

I blinked and swallowed. I was taken aback.

Because he was right.

Only it hadn't actually occurred to me until the moment Russell suggested it.

However, on other occasions, I have specifically set out with a theme in mind.

The theme of my book *The Seymour Tapes* (2005) – which is about a man who installs secret cameras in his house so he can see what his family say about him behind his back – came in the form of a question:

'Do you really want to know what you think you want to know?'

Or, to put it more simply, 'Curiosity killed the cat.'

The theme of my book *White City Blue* (1999) was also in the form of a question (themes often are).

That question was: 'What are friends *really* for?'

The identification of these themes helped me to write the books.

More specifically, they helped me decide what ought to happen next.

Because whatever was going to happen next in a scene, that scene ought to do at least some work to illustrate the theme.

Which at least narrowed down the field of possibilities somewhat.

(One of the main problems of writing a book is infinite possibility. So anything that makes things more limited is to be welcomed. The chaos of *anything*, finally, has to be turned into the finitude of *something*.)

ooooo

Along with theme, another thing that gives unity to the events in a story is *causality* – or what some theorists have called 'plot', which they distinguish from 'story'.

(I should mention at this point that later in this book I will ignore this distinction between 'story' and 'plot', and use the two words, for the main part, interchangeably.)

It was E. M. Forster, in *Aspects of the Novel* (1927), who first made the formal distinction between plot and story when he wrote:

> Let us define a plot. We have defined a story as a narrative of events arranged in their time-sequence. A plot is also a narrative of events, the emphasis *falling on causality* [my italics]. 'The king died and then the queen died' is a story. 'The king died, then the queen died of grief' is a plot. The time-sequence is preserved, but their sense of causality overshadows it. [Chapter 5: 'The Plot']

Nigel Watts embroiders the point in his book *Write a Novel: And Get It Published* (2010):

> Although a story may be interesting it is rarely as satisfying as a well-constructed plot. Why? Because without causality, there are usually no answers to the questions 'what happens next?' and 'how did we get into this mess?'
>
> Young children have no sense of plot. Listen to their stories: 'This happened and then this happened and then this…' Love them though we may, there is only so much prattle we can listen to before we tire… More than the events themselves, it is the *links* [my italics] we find compelling. [Chapter 2: 'Plot']

I should mention that there are plenty of writers who don't really worry too much about the governance of causality. These are novelists who prefer to write novels as a series of character sketches or disconnected scenes rather than as fully realised plots. These are more like interconnected short stories bound together into a single volume.

*Olive Kitteridge* (2008) by Elizabeth Strout is one of these, as is *Mrs Bridge* (1959) by Evan S. Connell. Karl Ove Knausgaard's 'novels' read exactly like life, rambling from one event to another with hardly any causal link at all over five entire volumes. There are many other examples.

You can get away with this – if you are a good enough writer of sentences and observer of character and scene.

Strout, Connell and Knausgaard definitely are good enough, because they are among the greatest writers of each of their generations.

But not many people are good enough.

A person with the ability to write a whole novel is rare. One who can do it successfully without bothering with a linked-up plot is bordering on a genius.

I would also contend that these writers *do* have plots in their work.

The thing is, they are *internal plots*.

The narrative is not defined by what happens in the outside world, but by what happens in the interior world.

And in the case of these writers – and other 'character-driven' texts – we see a definite development (or regression) of the characters as the novel progresses.

In other words, we have a character arc – which is a kind of psychological plot.

This is another reason why plot and character are two aspects of the same thing.

ooooo

In life, as we have observed, things tend to happen quite randomly. Causality is *involved*, but in a rather fragmented and unpredictable way.

I drink a glass of water. I brush my teeth. Then a pebble thrown up by a passing car shatters my window and I have to call the glazier.

The cause of my drinking a glass of water is thirst. The cause of my brushing my teeth is the need to stop decay. The cause of my calling a glazier is the accidental pebble.

And so on.

(Read Aristotle if you want a handy primer on the various orders of causality.)

My life comprises what you might call piecemeal, or even random, causality, with the occasional intrusion of chance. (The tooth-brushing and water-drinking are intentional; the pebble is accidental.)

My thirst and my brushing of teeth are not connected causally. They are connected to drinking water and the fear of tooth decay, respectively.

The broken window is connected to neither.

But the role of causality in a novel goes much further than the kind of scattergun causality found in real life.

It's not just present in the narrative, it *governs* the action, or, as Forster puts it, *overshadows* the time sequence.

It's not exactly ubiquitous, but it's a lot more present, intrusive and coherent than in real life.

In *A Swim in a Pond in the Rain*, George Saunders observes:

> There are two things that separate writers who go on to publish from those who don't.
>
> First, a willingness to revise.
>
> Second, the extent to which the writer has learned to make causality.
>
> *Causality to the writer is like melody to the songwriter* [my italics]. ['And Yet They Drove On: Thoughts on "Master and Man"']

Chance also appears in a novel, an event coming out of the blue as it were – but the further into a novel you get, the less chance should make an appearance.

If your novel is resolved by an outrageous coincidence, the reader is unlikely to believe in it.

The novel has to be resolved by the *outcome of all the causal actions that precede it*.

The *protagonist* in a novel is a person whose life is determined by a chain of cause-and-effect events deliberately created by the author, in order to elicit a response – perhaps intrigue, perhaps understanding, perhaps emotion – in the reader.

In the first scene of my first novel, *White City Blue*, the protagonist, Frankie Blue, meets someone with whom he falls in love, Veronica Tree.

Because he falls in love with her, he has to introduce her to his old (male) friends.

When friends and girlfriend meet they have, at best, ambivalent feelings about each other.

A difficult choice for Frankie arises when he finds out that Veronica's thirtieth birthday falls on the same day as the day that all his friends have, for years, ceremonially celebrated their long-standing friendship (the early intrusion of chance, usually more convincing narratively than its late appearance).

After much agonising, Frankie decides where his loyalties lie, rejects Veronica's pleas and chooses to spend the day with his friends rather than his girlfriend.

Because of that, Veronica leaves him.

Then, on the day of the celebration itself, the friends all fall out between themselves.

Because of that, Frankie is left alone – with neither friends nor fiancée.

Because of that, he now spends most of his spare time alone or with his mother.

Because of his enforced solitude, Frankie is given pause to examine what is most important to him in life.

Because of that, he begs Veronica to return.

Because of that – well, I won't spoil it for you.

But the principle is clear.

ooooo

The story-makers Pixar offer this formula when explaining story structure.

'Once upon a time there was... Every day... *One* day... Because of that... Because of that... Because of that... Until *finally*...'

Story structure is larger than causality, and we will deal with that in due course, but this template serves to illustrate some elements of the causal principle well enough.

Here is that Pixar template as applied to *Great Expectations* (1861).

*Once upon a time* there was an orphan, called Philip Pirrip – 'Pip'.

*Every day* Pip spends in the company of his beloved father figure, Joe, and his tartar of an aunt, Mrs Joe, with whom he lives, and readies himself for a life as a blacksmith.

*One day* he is invited to the house of a rich lady, Miss Havisham, where he meets a beautiful girl, Estella, with whom he falls in love, but who disdains him because of his coarseness and vulgarity.

*Because of that*, when offered the chance to advance himself he determines to become a gentleman and win the heart of Estella.

*Because of that* he goes to London to learn the manners of the well-bred.

*Because of that* he becomes something of a snob, proud and ambitious.

*Because of that* he is horrified when his benefactor is revealed not to be Miss Havisham, but a convict on the run – Magwitch, the feral creature who once accosted him terrifyingly on the marshes when he was a child.

*Because of* the arrival of the convict Magwitch, he begins to change and become more humble and compassionate. He stops thinking purely about himself. (And we learn that Pip's coming-into-fortune wasn't an accident at all.)

*Because of that* he helps Magwitch try to escape.

*Because of that* he finds inner completion.

*Because of that* Estella (who has gone on a similar journey from pride to humility) accepts him (at least, she does in one of the two endings Dickens wrote).

*And finally*, they come together.

ooooo

As well as theme and causality, a third function of plot is *purposefulness.*

Every scene in a plot should have a purpose. As should every act in every drama.

This purpose is usually to progress the action, develop the character or demonstrate the theme.

And always, hopefully, to entertain – or at least thoroughly engage – the reader.

Even if the scene is there mainly to provide entertainment it can't just be dropped in from nowhere.

There has to be a *reason for the scene.*

Otherwise, however engaging the scene might be, it shouldn't be in the book.

ooooo

So now we have some idea of what binds a plot together:

*Theme*
*Causality*
and
*Purposefulness*

With this established, we can turn to the shape of stories in more detail – otherwise known as *structure.*

## THE ANCIENT SECRET OF STORYTELLING: *Three-act structure*

*Three-act structure* is a centuries-old technique for developing a narrative in a way that will be interesting for the consumer of a story.

It's pretty simple (at first glance).

Beginning. Middle. End.

Act One. Act Two. Act Three.

This is the basis of classical drama, dating from the time of the great Athenian playwrights.

But how important is plot in the novel – a much more modern form of storytelling?

In a 2016 essay published in *New York Magazine* entitled 'Is It Story That Makes Us Read?', the writer Christian Lorentzen observed: 'There's something hostile to the bagginess of the novel in Aristotle's notion that the best works are those in which nothing can be subtracted without the meaning being lost.'

He was talking about the assertion from the *Poetics*, the urtext on storytelling, that if you can lift a part of the narrative out and the plot doesn't collapse, then it has no place in the story.

We cannot be that strict about the novel.

As Lorentzen observes, it is too baggy a construction.

But at the same time, understanding the principles of dramatic structure and narrative economy is crucial to the modern author.

At least if they want to keep the reader on board.

As George Saunders observes:

> We might think of a story as a candy factory... We expect everything in the place – every person, every phone, every department, every procedure – to be somehow related to, or 'about', or 'contributory to' that moment of candy-making...
>
> Or imagine we're bouncers, roaming through Club Story, asking each part, 'Excuse me, but why do you need to be in here?' In a perfect story, every part has a good answer. ['The Heart of the Story: Thoughts on "The Singers"']
>
> Don't make things happen for no reason... Having made something happen, make it matter. ['A Page at a Time: Thoughts on "In the Cart"']

Saunders was talking about short stories – a much tighter form than the novel, as is the drama or screenplay.

But it's a good principle for the novelist to apply – albeit within a slightly looser framework.

ooooo

Plots, you might say, are tidied-up versions of life.

Why are we attracted to the relative tidiness of plots in the first place?

We have already observed that life (story) is not the same as fiction (plot).

But – as a species of anxious, thinking animal – human beings don't much like this situation.

Life – *story* – is too disorderly to bear.

Which is why our minds are constantly trying to turn the randomness of life into a plot.

Into, as it were, a three-act structure.

In his essay on drama, *Three Uses of the Knife* (1998), David Mamet writes:

> Dramatic structure is not an arbitrary – or even a conscious – invention. It is an organic codification of the human mechanism for ordering information. Event, elaboration, denouement; thesis, antithesis, synthesis; boy meets girl, boy loses girl, boy gets girl; act one, two, three. [Chapter 3: '3 Uses of the Knife']

Our survival mechanism orders the world into

> cause – effect – conclusion... To create or witness drama [is] to order the universe into a comprehensible form. [Chapter 1: 'The Wind-Chill Factor']

Mamet was addressing himself to playwrights and screenwriters.

But the same principles apply to all storytellers – at least to some degree.

ooooo

The story theorist Tzvetan Todorov refers to the three stages of a story as 'equilibrium – disequilibrium – equilibrium'.

Psychologically it might be stated as follows: 'no knowledge – approaching knowledge – understanding and acceptance of knowledge'.

This simple pattern is found in most classic storytelling, be it St George and the Dragon (man leaves village, goes into cave and fights dragon, rescues virgin and returns to village), Jason and the Argonauts (man goes on journey, finds Golden Fleece, comes home again) or *Beowulf* (community threatened by monster, man goes to slay it, returns triumphant).

This is the three-act structure.

It's the perennial pattern of storytelling.

At this level, story structure is both obvious and commonsensical and will be immediately recognisable to anyone who goes to blockbuster movies, or enjoys classic novels, or indulges in pretty much any kind of mainstream entertainment.

The trouble starts when you begin to examine the three-act structure more closely.

And it gets worse the closer you look, especially when you try to break it down into smaller parts – as many people have done.

But it's still worth examining structure closely, since the three-act principle is at the heart of storytelling.

Because a plot or drama with a three-act structure is not some kind of random phantasm put there to annoy writers trying to complete novels.

It is simply a reverberation – through the medium of art – of the *necessary way our minds work.*

That is why it is so powerful – and inescapable.

Our minds are narration machines, and we constantly try to impose a logic on events and our thoughts and perceptions, and, therefore, to make causal connections.

So that our lives have beginnings, middles and ends.

Rather than just a chaotic series of events we experience constantly and don't know how to make sense of.

ooooo

We've come a long way since Aristotle and the *Poetics.*

Probably too far.

Because, if you think too much about story structure, you are likely to get more than a little bogged down – like story theorist Stanley Williams, who came up with the diagram in Figure 1: the 'Story Diamond'. This is what happens when

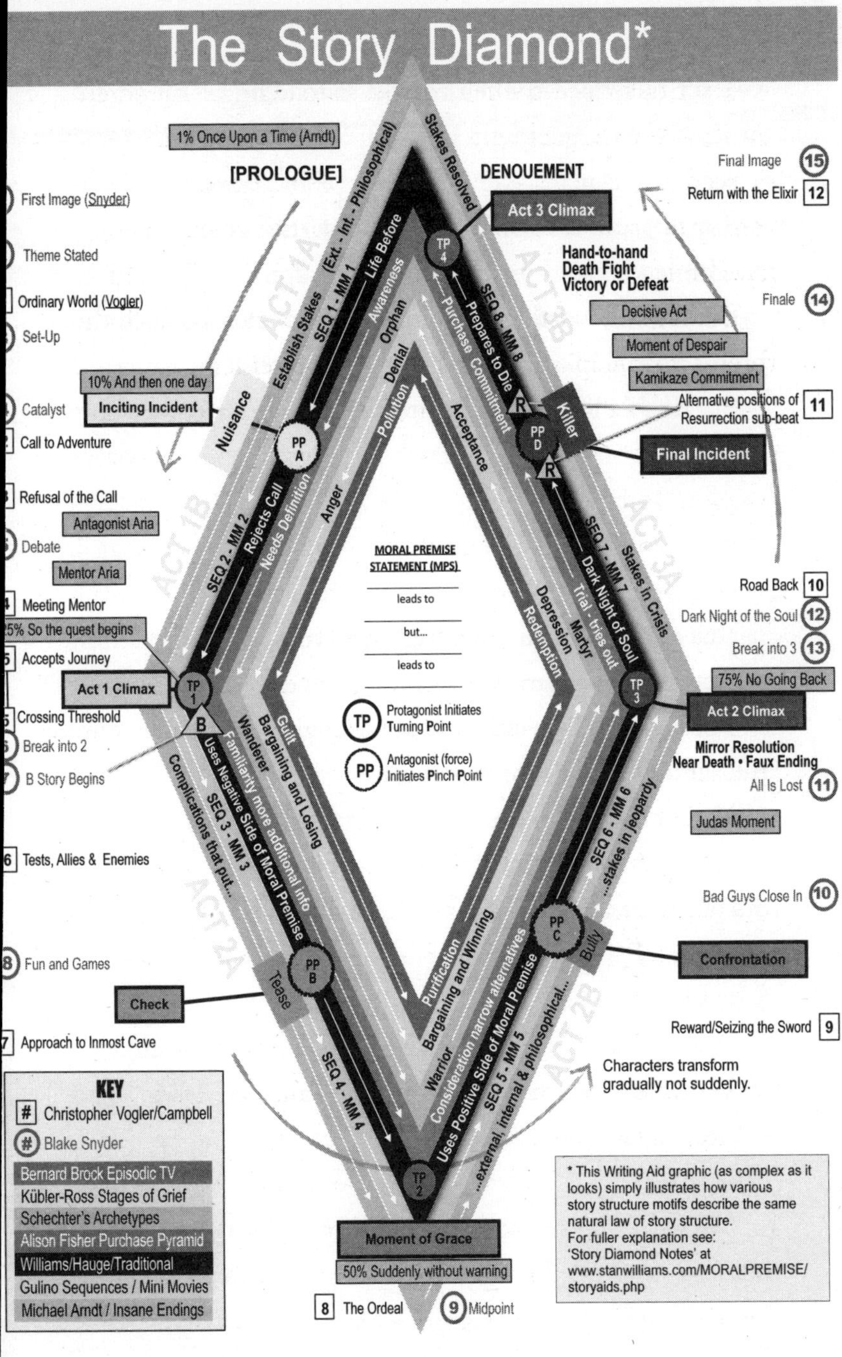

# The Story Diamond*

1% Once Upon a Time (Arndt)
[PROLOGUE]
DENOUEMENT
Final Image 15
Return with the Elixir 12
First Image (Snyder)
Theme Stated
Ordinary World (Vogler)
Set-Up
Stakes Resolved
(Ext. - Int. - Philosophical)
Establish Stakes
ACT 1A
SEQ 1 - MM 1
Life Before
Awareness
Orphan
Denial
Pollution
Act 3 Climax
TP 4
Hand-to-hand
Death Fight
Victory or Defeat
ACT 3B
SEQ 8 - MM 8
Prepares to Die
Purchase Commitment
Acceptance
Finale 14
Decisive Act
Moment of Despair
Kamikaze Commitment
Alternative positions of Resurrection sub-beat 11
10% And then one day
Catalyst
Inciting Incident
Call to Adventure
Nuisance
PP A
Killer
PP D
R
Final Incident
Refusal of the Call
Antagonist Aria
Debate
Mentor Aria
Meeting Mentor
ACT 1B
SEQ 2 - MM 2
Rejects Call
Needs Definition
Anger
MORAL PREMISE STATEMENT (MPS)
leads to
but...
leads to
Stakes in Crisis
ACT 3A
SEQ 7 - MM 7
Dark Night of Soul
Trial - tries out
Martyr
Depression
Redemption
Road Back 10
Dark Night of the Soul 12
Break into 3 13
25% So the quest begins
Accepts Journey
Act 1 Climax
TP 1
Crossing Threshold
Break into 2
B Story Begins
B
75% No Going Back
TP 3
Act 2 Climax
Mirror Resolution
Near Death • Faux Ending
All Is Lost 11
TP — Protagonist Initiates Turning Point
PP — Antagonist (force) Initiates Pinch Point
Complications that put...
SEQ 3 - MM 3
Uses Negative Side of Moral Premise
Familiarity more additional info
Wanderer
Guilt
Bargaining and Losing
Judas Moment
Tests, Allies & Enemies
SEQ 6 - MM 6
...stakes in jeopardy
Bad Guys Close In 10
ACT 2A
Fun and Games
PP B
Tease
Check
Purification
Bargaining and Winning
PP C
Bully
Confrontation
Consideration narrow alternatives
Warrior
Uses Positive Side of Moral Premise
SEQ 5 - MM 5
...external, internal & philosophical...
ACT 2B
Reward/Seizing the Sword 9
Approach to Inmost Cave
SEQ 4 - MM 4
Characters transform gradually not suddenly.

**KEY**
# Christopher Vogler/Campbell
(#) Blake Snyder
Bernard Brock Episodic TV
Kübler-Ross Stages of Grief
Schechter's Archetypes
Alison Fisher Purchase Pyramid
Williams/Hauge/Traditional
Gulino Sequences / Mini Movies
Michael Arndt / Insane Endings

TP 2
Moment of Grace
50% Suddenly without warning
8 The Ordeal
9 Midpoint

* This Writing Aid graphic (as complex as it looks) simply illustrates how various story structure motifs describe the same natural law of story structure.
For fuller explanation see:
'Story Diamond Notes' at
www.stanwilliams.com/MORALPREMISE/storyaids.php

FIGURE 1: Stanley D. Williams's 'Story Diamond'

you try to reduce the mystery of storytelling – an organic process – to a geometrical formula. (Williams, obviously a very clever man, spent his early career training NASA astronauts and car mechanics. And it kind of shows.)

But if you stick to the *basics*, and don't let yourself get carried away – and I know to my cost that it's a tempting rabbit hole – an understanding of simple act structure can be invaluable in creating a well-turned narrative.

ooooo

David Mamet has explained that the mind automatically parses reality into a three-act structure, and storytelling reflects that phenomenon.

An *act* is completed by a big *turning point* which spins the action off in a new direction.

A plot is made out of *acts* divided by *turning points*.

Or, to put it even more simply, as the agent Peggy Ramsay did when asked about 'this structure thing' by the playwright Alan Plater: 'Oh darling, it's just two or three little surprises followed every now and then by a bigger surprise.'

A 'surprise' is just another word for a turning point.

Other terms for a turning point include *crisis*, *critical choice*, *reversal*, *pinch point*, *peripeteia* or *subversion of expectation*.

(Story theorists like to come up with a bewildering number of terms for the same thing – or more or less the same thing.)

Story theorists also give names for BIG turning points. The *inciting incident*, the *call to adventure*, the *mid-point*, the *crisis*, the *final battle*, and so on.

But turning points are everywhere in a story, because they are units of change.

And stories *are* change (as you will see below in Chapter 3).

An act is made up of *scenes*.

If stories are all about change and the threat of change, then scenes are units of change within the act.

Acts culminate in major change.

Scenes show more minor changes embodied in individual moments or series of moments.

ooooo

John Yorke calls his book about storytelling *Into the Woods* (2013).

Behind his title is the idea that every story is, at heart, about a character or characters, like Hansel and Gretel, or Red Riding Hood, going 'into the woods' and then coming out again, usually armed with new understanding of themselves or of the world.

The mythologist Joseph Campbell similarly talked in *The Hero with a Thousand Faces* (1949) about how primary story characters go on a quest into what we might call the *void*.

This is a place where they are, in effect, neither here nor there.

The *void*, like the *woods*, is the crucible where the character has the potential to be transformed.

A classic story doesn't usually start *in* the woods – obviously.

Red Riding Hood is warned, before heading off from home to Grandma's, to keep to the safe path, that is, not to stray into the woods.

Hansel and Gretel start off as part of an (unhappy) family. It's their father who sends them into the woods, against their will.

So, a classic story usually starts with *stasis* – a place in the protagonist's life which is safe, predictable but often inauthentic or unsatisfactory in some way that the character may not be aware of.

Stasis – otherwise known as the *set-up* – represents the character before they enter the woods.

The set-up constitutes most of Act One.

During the first act *something happens* to disturb the stasis.

This something-that-happens is a turning point.

The first major turning point in a story is usually referred to as the *inciting incident*, *plot point one*, *crossing the threshold*, the *call to adventure* or *key event one*.

(As I say, story theorists love to come up with lots of partially interchangeable terms for the same thing.)

This change in the settled (though often unsatisfactory) condition of life is the turning point that propels us into Act Two.

Being lost in the void/woods is Act Two of a story.

Act Two, the longest act in any story, full of incident, adventures and reversals, ends, in classic storytelling, with another big turning point (the *crisis* or *worst point*).

After this, Act Three commences. The protagonist, after a *final battle* with the forces of antagonism – often embodied in the villain(s) – returns home, changed and more complete as a character.

('Home' is not necessarily a physical location, but the condition of wholeness that they lost at the beginning of the story.)

In most classic stories the character is changed by the time they reach the conclusion, but in other stories they may remain the same, sometimes having been asked to change by the dictates of the story – and failing.

(Tragic heroes, if they change at all, tend to change too late. Scarlett O'Hara is an example of the latter. So is King Lear.)

ooooo

As I have already implied, storytelling theory, even when it comes to something as apparently simple as the three-act structure, is something of a mess.

Identical things are called different names by different teachers and are sometimes placed differently in the sequence of events. And every teacher insists that their terms are the right ones and correctly locate the appropriate moments in a drama.

John Yorke came up with the diagram in Figure 2 to demonstrate the contradictory complexity of story theory. (He emphasises that such diagrams are ultimately fruitless.)

It charts all the different story structures as conceived of by various well-known story gurus.

You might call it 'Story Diamond 2: The Madness Continues'.

| | ONE | TWO | THREE | FOUR | FIVE |
|---|---|---|---|---|---|
| **TERENCE/ FREYTAG** | Set-up and call to action<br>Inciting incident | Things go well<br>Initial objectives achieved<br>Turning point | Things start to go wrong as forces of antagonism gather strength<br>Midpoint | Things go really badly wrong precipitating final confrontation with antagonist<br>Turning point/worst point | Overcoming flaw<br>Matters resolve for good or ill |
| **VLADIMIR PROPP** | Villainy or lack | Departure | Struggle<br>Victory<br>Midpoint<br>Liquidation | Return<br>Pursuit<br>Unrecognized Arrival | Difficult Task<br>Marriage |
| **JOSEPH CAMPBELL** | Innocent<br>Call to world of adventure<br>Childhood separation | Refusal of call<br>Supernatural aid | Crossing threshold<br>Atonement With father<br>Midpoint<br>Apotheosis | Refusal of the return<br>Magic flight | Rescue<br>Freedom to live<br>Master of two worlds |
| **MAUREEN MURDOCK*** | Separation from feminine<br>Identification with masculine | Road of trials<br>2-headed dragon<br>Slaying the ogre | Illusory boon<br>Initiation and descent to goddess<br>Midpoint<br>Yearning to connect with feminine | Wild woman<br>Healing | Integrating the feminine<br>Beyond duality |

| | ONE | TWO | THREE |
|---|---|---|---|
| **SYD FIELD** | Set up | Confrontation<br>Pinch Point<br>Pinch Point | Climax and resolution |

| | ONE | TWO | THREE | FOUR | FIVE |
|---|---|---|---|---|---|
| **VOGLER** | Ordinary world<br>Call to adventure | Reluctance or refusal of call<br>Encouragement by mentor | Crossing 1st threshold<br>Supreme ordeal<br>Reward<br>Midpoint<br>Tests allies enemies | Pursuit on the road back<br>3rd threshold<br>Death | Resurrection<br>Return with elixir |
| **BLAKE SNYDER** | Opening image<br>Set-up<br>Theme stated<br>Catalyst<br>Inciting incident | Debate<br>B-Story<br>Break into Act Two | Fun and games<br>Midpoint<br>Bad guys close in | All is lost<br>Dark Night of the Soul | Break into last act<br>Finale<br>Final image |
| **JOHN TRUBY** | Need/ Desire<br>1st reversal | Plan<br>1st Counter-attack | Drive<br>Seeming defeats<br>2nd reversal | Audience revelation by ally<br>3rd reversal | Battle<br>Moral decison<br>New equilib-rium |

| | ONE | TWO | THREE | FOUR | FIVE | SIX | SEVEN | EIGHT |
|---|---|---|---|---|---|---|---|---|
| **FRANK DANIEL†** | Status quo | The external want made explicit | Exploring the new world | 1st big test overcome | Forces gathering | Hitting the wall | Desperate action | Success and aftermath |
| **LINDA ARONSON** | Normality Disturbance Protagonist Plan Surprise Obstacle | | | | Complications<br>Sub-stories | More complications | and Obstacles | Climax<br>Resolution |

| **CHRISTOPHER BOOKER** | | | | |
|---|---|---|---|---|
| Call to action | Dream | Frustration | Nightmare | Matters resolved |

| **MICHAEL HAUGE** | | | | | |
|---|---|---|---|---|---|
| 1 Set-up | 2. New situation | 3. Progress | 4. Complications & higher stakes | 5. Final push | 6. Aftermath |

FIGURE 2: John Yorke's 'Lightning Guide to Screenwriting Gurus'

In my view, you cannot reduce storytelling to a series of exact named 'points' or stages.

You can't even be precise about where they lie in any particular sequence.

Yet, enticingly and unavoidably – there *is* a universal pattern in there somewhere.

And it's a pattern worth searching for – because it can help us with that most torturous of questions: 'What happens next?'

ooooo

An understanding of structure *is* useful – *if kept in its place*, that is, at the back of the mind rather than at the front, a shimmery watermark rather than a solid, heavily inked and overly complicated map.

Complicated maps are to be avoided because they are purely conscious inventions – and writing is a transaction between the conscious and the unconscious mind.

A worthwhile novel cannot be written consciously, because it would be dead.

And if written completely unconsciously, then you get *On the Road.*

Which is fine, if you are Jack Kerouac.

But you're not.

And even if you were, it would be too late now to try that particular experiment.

ooooo

I dislike structure diagrams.

However – after reading all the texts on the subject, and after many days and hours of experimenting, and talking to story theorists, I eventually devised my own diagram illustrating plot structure.

As far as I'm concerned, it's as simple as it can possibly be rendered.

It covers ground we haven't explored yet – we are still on three-act structure – but you might find it useful to have at hand as we move through the various complications.

It is laid out in Appendix 1.

Meanwhile, here's a diagram of basic three-act structure – storytelling at its simplest (Figure 3).

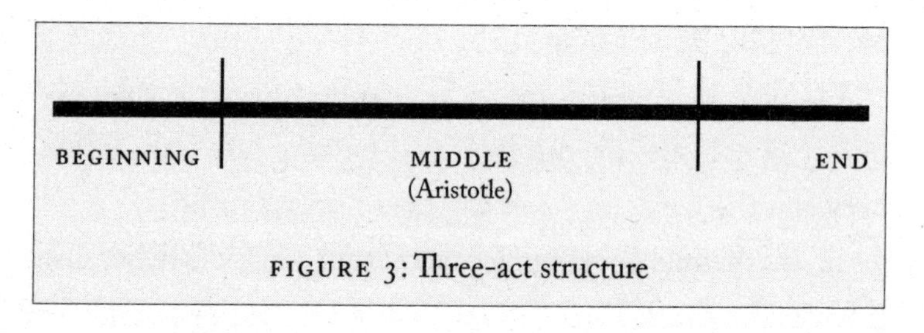


FIGURE 3: Three-act structure

The two vertical lines represent turning points – key moments of change.

The only other thing worth noting at this point is that the middle is much longer than the beginning or the end.

Here's a concrete example of a story in three acts.

### ACT ONE

A man walks along a road. He falls into a hole (*turning point*).

### ACT TWO

He is trapped there and struggles to escape in a variety of largely unsuccessful ways that test his mettle. He comes to a low point when he gives up all hope. But he musters his resources and decides to keep going despite everything (*turning point*).

### ACT THREE

He gets out again.

ooooo

It's at this point we can no longer avoid the question of how plot is linked with character.

It is linked through the principle of *change*.

But before we examine how change operates in a work of fiction, let's do an initial examination of how *character* works.

# 2

# *Character (Part One)*

## INTRODUCTION TO CHARACTER:
### *How to create an artificial person*

What is a fictional character?

A character is a symbol for a person, just as a word is a symbol for a concept.

Why is it a symbol?

Because a real person is far too complex to depict.

To portray even a single human being accurately would take an infinitely long book and an author possessed of an impossible level of genius.

A fictional character can therefore be best described as a *sincere approximation* of a real person.

As the story theorist James Frey remarks: '*Homo Fictus* is an abstraction meant to communicate the essence, not the totality of *Homo Sapiens*.'

A storyteller can only show a tiny sliver of the reality of the human soul – but they can at least show it authentically.

That scrap is enough to interest us, even compel us, because it reflects something within us – the consumers of the story.

If it doesn't reflect anything in us that we can recognise, it is sterile.

A fictional character is therefore necessarily partial and incomplete.

And would be even if we knew exactly what a person *was* in the first place.

Yet this same awkward fact – that we don't know – means that drama, and storytelling, are bestowed with a function.

Because an attempt to address the finally unanswerable problem 'what is a person?' goes to the heart of all fiction and drama.

Or at least all *good* fiction or drama.

In his book *The Science of Storytelling* (2019), Will Storr refers to this problem as 'the dramatic question'.

'If there's a single secret to storytelling,' he writes,

> then I believe it's this. *Who is this person?* Or, from the perspective of the character, *Who am I?* It's the definition of drama. It is its electricity, its heartbeat, its fire.
>
> Harnessing the energy of the dramatic question means understanding that the answer is not easily found. This is because, even at the best of times, most of us don't actually know who we are...
>
> The dramatic question has the power to unfold so unexpectedly and endlessly because the protagonists

themselves don't know the answer. They're discovering who they are, moment by moment, as the pressure of the drama is applied. [Chapter 3: 'The Dramatic Question']

## CHARACTER STUDIES

### *Character vs characterisation*

A fully formed fictional character typically has two elements – *character* and *characterisation.*

It is *character* that the writer who aspires to any depth is concerned with, although it is worth briefly defining *characterisation* first.

*Characterisation* is the visible characteristics of a fictional character. Their age, education, style of dress, job, whether they are quiet and apologetic or aggressive and bullying. Things you can know by observation.

It's the outside appearance of someone. What they look like. Their biography. Their likes and dislikes. Their past. Their upbringing.

It's surface information.

Characters who only have characterisation to define themselves will be able to meet Aristotle's definition of character as 'repeated action'.

They will perform a number of habitual actions and gestures that mean we recognise the character across time – a character that remains more or less stable throughout the drama (even if their chief characteristic is instability).

In this sense, Jean Brodie in Muriel Spark's *The Prime of Miss Jean Brodie* (1961) – while one of literature's greatest creations – is more characterisation than character.

Purely characterised characters are often, although not always (as Jean Brodie demonstrates), minor players in a drama.

More often, we don't know them very well and we're not terribly interested in knowing them any better.

A characterised minor character can still be well realised. You need very few brushstrokes to get a static portrait walking, as this telling little sketch from Maupassant demonstrates (as cited by James Wood in *How Fiction Works*):

> He was a gentleman with red whiskers who always went first through a doorway.

You don't have to give much in the way of character traits to the postman who delivers the letter telling the protagonist that their husband has left them. Perhaps he walks with a limp and his hair sticks up on end. That at least renders him something more than a generic postman.

But you do have to have some idea of the sort of person it is who receives the letter – if they are the main figure in the story.

The depiction of this person, the protagonist, is the territory of character.

*Character* is the internal aspect of a fictional person.

This is the subject of focus for the storyteller who has any ambitions for depth. They will strip away, action by action, choice by choice, always under pressure, characterisation to reveal character.

Under pressure – because true character only really emerges when put under pressure.

It is in extreme circumstances through which we find out who we really are, or what we are capable of, and who the people around us really are – or are capable of.

We are what we do, not what we say.

The key fact for writers is this:

*People are not what they seem to be.*

'There's the mask outside, inside there's the one you're working on,' as Robert McKee put it in a lecture.

Nobody's the same on the inside as out.

ooooo

A satisfying main character, although fictional and limited, will share many of the central characteristics of a real person.

So what is the inner core of a person?

No one is quite sure, but I play a game with my students by simply asking them outright, 'What is a person?'

Bear in mind I ask them to come up with universal human characteristics, rather than individual quirks (which are necessarily also part of a fictional character).

Below are a few of the answers they have come up with over the years.

(Obviously, some of these categories would not apply to people with personality disorders such as psychopathy.)

*A person has a moral sense.*

*A person makes mistakes.*

*A person has a dark side, often hidden from themselves.*

*A person has created their own private (imaginary) world which they seek to defend.*

*A person has desires.*

*A person has secrets.*

*A person has a past – and memory of the past, which may or may not be accurate.*

*A person has fears – both universal and individual.*

*A person is divided, that is, in conflict with themselves and the world.*

Some will argue that such lists are meaningless, that human character is mutable, containing limitless plasticity and changing perpetually according to history, environment and culture.

I don't agree.

My view is that of William Faulkner: 'Human nature is the only subject that doesn't date.'

If I didn't believe this, I could scarcely find a motivation to write, for I would have nothing to say – except 'I have nothing to say.'

One can argue with the definitions that my students came up with, and add to them, probably indefinitely, but it doesn't really matter exactly how you frame the answer to the problem.

The point is that you, as a writer, must identify *your* idea of what universal human characteristics are and build at least some of them into your character (along with individual characteristics, which spring from, or accompany, these fundamentals).

I have lost count of the number of student texts I have considered where I have no interest in the character because they don't consistently display, or act according to, at least some of the central traits suggested in the above list.

Having made a brief, and admittedly crude, attempt to define a person, there are some (obvious) remarks worth making that are also helpful in designing a fictional character.

The first is that some characters in a story are more significant than others.

Which leads us to…

## *The protagonist*

The word *protagonist* literally means 'the person who struggles'.

The most important character in a drama is the protagonist.

The protagonist is the person in whom we are most interested, who represents us in the form of an avatar; that is, they are the character we most identify with.

As McKee put it in one of his lectures, the cast is a solar system, and the protagonist is the sun.

The cast are held together by the gravitational pull of the star at the centre.

The protagonist, in that sense, creates all the other characters.

The other characters service the character of the protagonist.

It is the character of the protagonist we are primarily concerned with as writers, although a story may have several or multiple protagonists. But once a character is designated 'a protagonist' then the writer has to start thinking deeply about what sort of character they are.

They are no longer merely the postman or the man with the red beard.

The same applies to all characters who have a major part in the drama, including the antagonist (unless you are writing a villain in a *Scooby-Doo* cartoon).

So what are the key characteristics that the protagonist should display?

That depends to some extent on whether they are one-, two- or three-dimensional characters.

### *Dimensions of character*

Protagonists in a novel are unlikely to be one-dimensional because one-dimensional characters are too simple, that is, they have only one characteristic that defines them.

Perhaps they are always angry, say, or always nice, or always loyal, like Mrs Micawber, who 'never will desert Mr Micawber'.

But they do not have enough ammunition to fight the war

that a protagonist must engage in during the construction of a narrative.

*Two-dimensional* characters, or 'flat' characters (as E. M. Forster christened them), were known as 'humours' in the seventeenth century.

Now we know them as 'types', or caricatures.

They may have more than one single idea or quality, but these qualities are fixed.

Miss Jean Brodie, Becky Sharp and Jay Gatsby are all rather flat even though they have a range of personality traits and are central to their stories.

They are, in other words, predictable.

'The test of a round character is whether it is capable of surprising in a convincing way,' writes Forster. A flat character 'never surprises'.

I'm not knocking two-dimensional characters.

A two-dimensional character can be a perfectly satisfying one who can carry us through from the beginning to the end of a lengthy narrative.

Writing in two dimensions isn't necessarily a failure. Far from it.

Two dimensions versus three dimensions can be seen to represent the tragic versus the dynamic view of life.

Comedy is (paradoxically) tragic, which is why Larry David never changes in *Curb Your Enthusiasm*.

Jean Brodie, as I have already noted, is simply a collection of repeated phrases: 'the *crème de la crème*'; 'I am in my prime'; 'the Philistines are upon us, Mr Lloyd'.

The device works because we only ever see Jean Brodie as a schoolgirl might, in two dimensions – never at home or by herself.

Limiting the character makes it powerful, because it is realistic – from the point of view of her pupils (and it's her pupils who are, in a sense, the real protagonists).

There is a second element to two-dimensional characters, other than having *multiple*, but *limited*, personality traits (perhaps this is why they are conceived of as having two dimensions).

Two-dimensional characters *do not change* by the end of the story.

Jean Brodie does not change.

Superman never changes, nor does James Bond (at least in their original incarnations).

Yet these are all great characters.

Nearly all of Dickens's characters are 'flat' – according to E. M. Forster's rather unkind assessment. (I would suggest that, at the heart of his greatest book, *Great Expectations*, is a fully fledged, undeniably three-dimensional character, Philip Pirrip. So is Scrooge three-dimensional, for that matter.)

But it didn't stop him from being one of our greatest novelists.

Eddie Carbone in Arthur Miller's *A View from the Bridge* is unable to change, although the events of the story demand it of him.

It is this *inability to change under pressure* that renders him a fascinating tragic hero – and yet, at the same time, a two-dimensional one.

Comedy in particular relies heavily on two-dimensional characters.

Basil Fawlty or Father Ted never change.

It is their inability to change that makes them funny.

Tom and Jerry never change. Mr Bean never changes.

(It's not an iron rule. The characters in the wonderful TV comedy *Brooklyn Nine-Nine* do change. Or at least some of them do. At least by the end of the series.)

The enjoyment comes from us watching them get into trouble over and over again because of this central flaw, which they themselves are unaware of.

For the many two-dimensional characters, it is the world around them, or their understanding of that world, or the audience/reader's understanding of that world, that changes, rather than their inner selves.

It is a change that has been carefully worked out as meaningful by the author.

But *change there must be*, otherwise there is no story.

A *three-dimensional* character is primarily a character that undergoes a change during the arc of a story.

If the character is three-dimensional, if they want something, they're going to have to change to get it.

*All drama is built on change.*

I will shortly demonstrate this concretely – with the story I invented about a man who literally gets into a hole and then gets out again.

But before that – some reflections on the nature of *change* in storytelling.

# 3

# *How Character and Plot Are Unified through Change*

On the first page of the first chapter of my novel *Rumours of a Hurricane* (2002), I wrote this sentence (which amounts to an authorial statement):

> The secret truth is this: that things change. That things *are* change.

It was the opening of a story, but it might have been the opening of a book *about* story.

Here's John Yorke, from *Into the Woods*:

> Change is the bedrock of life and consequently the bedrock of narrative. [Chapter 4: 'The Importance of Change']
>
> All dramatic structure is built on the chassis of change. [Chapter 9: 'Scenes']

And David Corbett, in *The Art of Character* (2013):

> The key element of story, which is a dramatic form, is that in a story *something changes*. [Chapter 18: 'The Challenge of Change: Three Protagonist Questions']

So why are we so fascinated by change?

(And it *is* fascination. As John Yorke notes: 'the image every TV director in fact or fiction looks for is the close-up of the human face as it registers change.')

David Corbett suggests an answer:

> Change remains one of the most baffling aspects of our existence. The mind, so entranced by images and ideas and names, naturally seeks to anchor itself in some notion of solidity. But the stuff of life won't hold still.
>
> Stories that capture this tension... strike at a key truth of our existence. [Chapter 18: 'The Challenge of Change: Three Protagonist Questions']

Change is not only fascinating.

It is what we need to prosper in life. Will Storr:

> Change is... an opportunity... Change is hope. Change is promise. It's our winding path to a more successful tomorrow. [Chapter 1: 'Creating a World']

Unfortunately – given Will's premise – humans are programmed to *avoid change*.

Lisa Cron, in her book *Story Genius*, writes:

> No matter how dearly we want something, avoiding change is our middle name. That's probably why the only thing that causes us to change, internally or otherwise, is an unavoidable *external* force… a problem we can't dodge, duck, or deflect is barreling straight toward us, giving us no choice but to take action… story is about change, and we're wired to avoid change. Ask us to change, and we reach for the 'opt out' button… Change, even good change, is so damn hard.
>
> As your novel begins, your protagonist has most likely spent a good bit of time downplaying, postponing, and often willfully ignoring the urge to change. [Chapter 8: 'The When']

Change compels us – and it terrifies us.

Will Storr:

> Identifying and accepting our flaws, and then changing who we are, means breaking down the *very structure of our reality* before rebuilding it in a new and improved form. This is not easy. It's painful and disturbing. We'll often fight with all we have to resist this kind of profound change. [Chapter 2: 'The Flawed Self']

ooooo

So – we are caught in a paradox.

We need change. Life demands it of us.

But, all too frequently, we don't want it, or we can't accept it.

That's why all stories show how and why life changes.

This is the grand reason why we tell stories – to equip us to live.

Stories can be thought of as psychological flight simulators to examine and practise change.

They are 'a road map of change', as John Yorke would have it.

In a classic story, the road map of change represents the protagonist's growing knowledge of their own flaws, their gradual acceptance, prevarication, then total rebirth.

Or, in a tragedy, their final destruction or self-destruction.

Stories that ignore change – at some level – are sterile.

The author Lajos Egri remarked that 'the only place where characters defy natural law and fail to change is in the realm of bad writing'.

ooooo

When constructing a story, story theorists talk about 'story events'.

These are different from life events, just as a plot is different from a story and a fictional character is different from a real person.

In a lecture, Robert McKee defined a story event as a 'meaningful *change* in the value-charged condition of a character's life, achieved through conflict'.

Conflict – because it's only through pressure that people change.

Story events are moments of meaningful change, or that lead to meaningful change (or *demand* meaningful change).

Meaningful because a change – in the context of a story – is not just, say, a change in the weather.

Even the worst-written story will inevitably have change of some sort. There may be a great deal of change – car crashes, murders, screaming arguments, what have you.

But if the change is *meaningless*, then there is no drama.

The question is – is the change meaningful, is the change unified into a structure and a theme?

The change we are looking for is a change in the *values* of the character – or at least, pressure on those values from an external source (that is, plot).

It is a change in the character's attitudes, or mentality, or morality, or world view.

Or, if you prefer, their soul.

Or, as we have already observed, it may be their *inability* to change that compels us as readers.

David Corbett:

> Though it might be said that the motives or behavior of such characters don't appreciably change, their *emotions*, *insight* or *attitude toward life* does by story's

> end. If not, that *refusal* to embrace the opportunity for change is felt by the reader...
>
> [In such cases] change isn't impossible, it's forsaken – meaning a decision *not to change* has been made.
>
> And *a decision is inherently dramatic.* [Chapter 18: 'The Challenge of Change: Three Protagonist Questions']

ooooo

A scene in a drama, McKee writes, is 'an action through conflict in more or less continuous time and space that turns the value-charged condition of a character's life on at least one value with a degree of perceptible significance'.

Scenes are built through a sequence of 'beats' (or moments) and lead to an *act climax* (the *inciting incident*, the *mid-point* or the *crisis*), which represents *major change*, that is, a particularly significant turning point for the protagonist.

The story climax is absolute and irreversible – after it, no more change is possible.

A fictional story – including a novel – is simply a 'massive story event', since it represents change right across the arc of the story.

That is what is meant by the 'dramatic arc'.

ooooo

Why else are stories so concerned with change?

Because change is inherently dramatic.

Why?

Because change – at least internal change – involves doubt, prevarication and choice.

We are faced all day, every day, with choices that are unavoidable.

Many of those choices are insignificant. Others have more weight. Still others have the potential to be life-altering – and with them comes the promise of a new adventure, or the threat of regret.

It is these last choices that the storyteller is usually most concerned with.

There are certainly, as we have already noted, characters who *do not* change during the course of a novel. The detective who has to discover the truth about a crime, for instance.

Instead of a flaw, they have a deficiency of knowledge, which they have to overcome during the story.

It's still a change. And change there must be. A change that can exist at many levels.

Will Storr describes plot as 'a symphony of change'.

The plot changes. The character changes.

And, furthermore:

> The characters' understanding of their situation can change. The characters' plan for achieving their goal can change. The characters' goal can change. A character's understanding of themselves can change. A character's

> understanding of their relationships can change. The reader's understanding of who the character is can change… And so on. [Chapter 4: 'Plots, Endings and Meaning']

You can plot these changes onto some of the turning points described in story structure – but the exact placing of them is not so important as understanding that change is constantly unfolding.

Let's see some of this change play out in a fictional story which combines both character and plot.

Not perhaps in a symphony of change so much – but in a simple tune.

# 4

# *'Charlie and the Hole': A Three-Act Story Incorporating Character and Plot*

I'm going to try to design a simple plot according to the three-act structure.

It will incorporate the pressure the plot puts on character, and how the character changes as a result.

(Although its simplicity actually makes it quite complex to design. I have rewritten and redrafted the story that follows dozens of times before it reached its current – still very basic – form.)

Don't worry for the moment about how realistic the plot is. You can pick holes (no pun intended) in it on a number of levels.

It's not there to make the short story of the year.

It's there to demonstrate an *idea*.

The action/character development you are about to read falls into the pattern described in Figure 4.

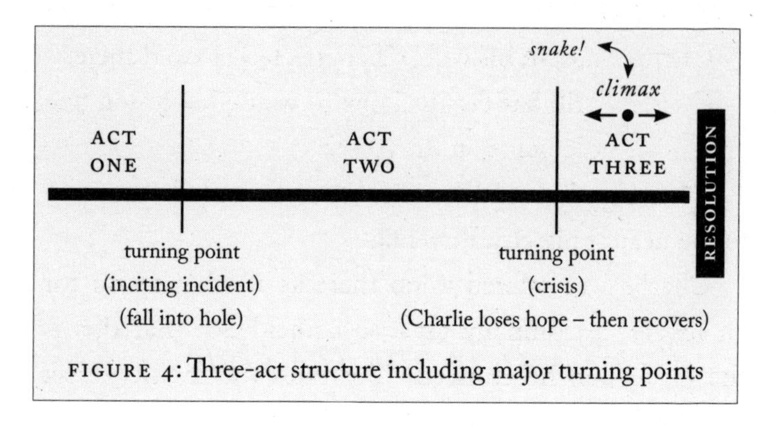


FIGURE 4: Three-act structure including major turning points

Let's invent a protagonist and give him a name.

Let's call him Charlie.

And let's give him some *character* aspects and a *problem* (one that exists *before* he acquires the fresh problem of falling into a hole).

Charlie happens to live in a small town in a part of the American wilderness – let's say Arizona – built around a complex of old mineshafts.

Sinkholes in this town – Sinkhole, Arizona – have been known to open up in the ground and swallow people whole.

Danger spots have been roped off, but there is always the risk that one has escaped the notice of the not-very-efficient authorities.

This is not the only unusual element of Charlie's surroundings.

They happen to be more heavily populated with rattle-snakes than just about anywhere else in America.

Both he and his wife – who is part Native American – grew up in the town.

Charlie hates it; his wife, Charlene, feels rooted there.

Charlene still has family living in wattle houses on one of the old settlements on the mesas.

After Charlie and Charlene were married, they moved to the nearest big city, Phoenix.

Charlie was offered a job there as a risk assessor for an insurance company. (It's no coincidence that this is the profession he chose. It illustrates the theme – risk aversion.)

Now, fifteen years later, they have moved back to Sinkhole from the city because Charlene, following the death of her father, has inherited a house in the town that belonged to her ancestors.

Charlie's widowed mother, who lives nearby, is still alive. She's widowed because Charlie's father died underground in a mining accident twenty years previously. She is delighted when Charlie returns as she is ailing. (She has been 'ailing' for the last decade in the hope of guilting Charlie back to Sinkhole.)

Charlie's problem (and it was a problem even before he returned to this backwater) is that he is by nature a very fearful person.

(Stories usually start with, or develop, a problem to be solved or a question to be answered, or both. George Saunders: 'We might imagine structure as a form of call-and-response. A question arises organically from the story and then the story, very considerately, answers it. If we want to make good structure, we just have to be aware of what question we are causing the reader to ask, then answer that question. The writer creates a set of expectations then responds to those expectations.')

Charlie was scared to leave Sinkhole when they originally moved to Phoenix, he was scared to leave the city to come and live back in this small town, he was scared to say no to his wife when she suggested moving back here, and, now he's here, he's perpetually scared of holes (remember what happened to his father) and snakes (part of his backstory is that he was bitten by a snake as a child and nearly died).

But even when he was in Phoenix, he was always nervous that he was going to be mugged or run over.

His fear leaves him not living the life he could live – if he were more resolute and courageous.

So those are the basics of Charlie's character.

Let's observe the action unfold as this character/plot helix plays out in a 'man in hole' plot with Charlie at the centre of it, in a three-act form.

## ACT ONE

To build Charlie's character, we need some more *exposition* – the imparting of necessary information which will get the story grounded.

We show Charlie about to leave his home – his wife's ancestral dwelling – in Sinkhole.

The landscape around is beautiful and wild, but desolate.

Today he's got to go out of town, into the wilderness that surrounds the settlement, in order to enquire about a job for an insurance company who have an office on an isolated enterprise park five miles away.

He doesn't believe that he can get the job. Charlie is timid and lacks confidence.

But he and Charlene need the money, since a letter has arrived that morning telling them that the house is about to be repossessed because the couple have fallen behind with their repayments on the home (Charlene inherited it with a mortgage attached).

(This is called *raising the stakes* or *increasing jeopardy*. It can also be termed *escalation*. Here's George Saunders again: 'What transforms a story from an anecdote is escalation.')

Charlie, this morning, is immaculately well dressed and tidy for his job interview.

(Perhaps because of his fear of chaos, another part of Charlie's character is that he hates dirt and thinks that if there is a spot of grime on him, he will never get the job.)

Before he leaves, he has a row with Charlene, who tells him that if he doesn't get the job this time (since their move into the boondocks he has been unemployed) their marriage will be on the rocks. And they'll probably lose the house.

In other words, still more jeopardy for Charlie.

Charlene tells him – and not for the first time – that he is too risk-averse, and that his lack of self-confidence is holding him back. She had to nag him into trying for this job in the first place, because Charlie thought he would only get rejected. Charlene complains bitterly that Charlie is scared of everything.

Just before Charlie leaves he notices a large worm on the kitchen floor (worms grow big in this part of America).

Charlie – who is long-sighted on top of everything else – thinks at first glance that it is a snake and starts, violently. But once he puts on his glasses, he can see that it is only a worm.

Not that he likes worms in the slightest, because they remind him of snakes.

His wife asks him to pick it up and get rid of it, but he won't because of his snake fear.

She casually picks up the worm and feigns throwing it at Charlie. He cringes in terror.

Contemptuously, she throws it out of the window, tells him he is pathetic and shoos him out.

He heads forlornly for the job interview – hours early, because, remember, he is highly risk-averse – worried that really he is the man Charlene says he is.

A loser, terrified of worms, terrified of holes, terrified of failing.

Just generally terrified.

So poor, beleaguered Charlie, permeated with flaws and anxieties of one kind or another, trudges off to his car.

Charlie gets in the car and starts to drive towards the insurance office along a single-track dirt road.

After half a mile the car stops.

He forgot to fill it with gas – as, it happens, he promised Charlene he would do the day before.

She is going to be mad with him.

So he's not going to go back to the house and tell her his problems.

She's not the only one who's going to be mad.

He has promised his perpetually ailing mother that he will drop in on the way to the interview and see how she is.

His phone is unable to pick up a signal so he can't ring anyone to explain.

He has to get to the interview. If he gets the job, Charlene will forgive him for not refilling the car with gas, he decides.

As for his mother, well, he'll have to take the hit.

The insurance people have told him to drop in at any time during the day – they are a pretty free-and-easy company, and it is only meant to be an initial meet-and-greet.

It is not yet 9 a.m.

There are no buses.

He decides he has no choice but to walk.

It is only five miles.

Charlie starts to walk away from the road in the direction of the insurance office, carefully brushing the dust of the desert from the hems of his formerly pristine trousers. Which, somewhat symbolically, are growing increasingly grubby.

ooooo

How do we show rather than tell that Charlie is risk-averse?

As we see him walk across the barren fields heading towards the insurance office, we see that he is constantly scanning the ground at his feet – despite the fact that, above him, it's a beautiful sunny day.

So he doesn't see the lovely hot-air balloons that happen to be floating above him in the sky.

Or the gorgeous birds that are perched in the scattered trees above him.

Or the elegant cloud formations.

Or the distant giant mesas – extraordinary rock formations – that loom in the distance.

He just compulsively looks at the ground through his indispensable thick-lens spectacles.

Watching for holes.

Or, perhaps, snakes.

ooooo

After about half an hour of trudging, and watching the ground obsessively...

BANG!

A massive sinkhole opens up under his feet and Charlie falls into it.

It's one of the old abandoned mineshafts which have been left unmarked.

His fall into the hole marks the end of Act One and the beginning of Act Two.

He has effectively fallen into a *turning point.*

Charlie has entered a new world which he is not accustomed to and which he fears.

He has acquired a new, urgent (if superficial and short-term) *desire.*

*To get out of the hole.*

In this story, he has to get out of not only the physical hole he has fallen into but the metaphorical hole of his fears.

Falling into the hole represents the awakening of the *forces of antagonism.*

The forces of antagonism can be people, inner psychological states, organisations, communities or a combination of these.

From this moment on, the protagonist (Charlie) is trying to restore the balance of life which has been upset – either by moving forward into dangerous but promising territory (good) or by retreating to the point he started from (bad).

The turning point (or inciting incident) often represents the first important choice the protagonist has to make in any story.

But, in this case, Charlie has no choice to make.

He just falls into the hole.

## ACT TWO

Act Two is the longest, most complicated and most problematic of acts.

It involves what Robert McKee calls 'progressive complications'.

This long act will feature scenes which involve conflict, threat, jeopardy, adventure – trials that escalate and become more intense and hazardous (*raising the stakes*).

The hole that Charlie has fallen into represents 'the void' (or 'the woods').

He is in unknown territory and doesn't know what the hell to do about it.

The scenes in Act Two will be governed by a series of *mini-goals* or *sub-goals*, all moving towards the conclusion, the *overarching goal*, the *superobjective*, driven by the protagonist's *desire* (to get out of the hole).

(He has other desires – to save his marriage, to get the job – but this is the one that concerns him overwhelmingly at the moment.)

Some mini-goals will be achieved; some mini-goals will not; some will move the protagonist further away from the overarching goal, some will move him closer – but there will always be some sort of general impulse towards forward movement.

What is important is that things *do not remain static.*

In other words, things must change.

If the mini-goal is not achieved, or there is a setback, then the protagonist has to try another way of getting what they want.

It is this tension between success and failure as the protagonist tries to move towards their goal which engages the attention of the reader or viewer.

There will be a constant shifting between positive and negative.

Every failure will induce greater effort, and involve (possibly) the temptation to give up or go back.

During this second act, the protagonist is typically tempted to return to the safe but unsatisfactory world from which they came (playing it safe and doing nothing, or following old, redundant strategies), while slowly, painfully, learning that there is another, better way of being, a place where valuable lessons may be learned and a new self awaits.

ooooo

So – Act Two of the story continues:

Charlie, after overcoming his initial shock, dusts himself down and, trying to suppress his panic, immediately attempts to climb out of the hole.

It's only twenty feet or so. Not as bad as it might have been. He can still easily make it to the insurance office.

It's easier than he thinks.

In less than a minute of scrambling up the wall of the hole, he's close to the top.

Muddy and tired, but basically OK.

But just as he pulls himself over the lip of the hole he slips on some mud and falls back down again.

As he falls, his glasses slip off – and they sink into a hole in the mud.

Charlie cannot retrieve them.

Angry and frustrated, and back where he started at the bottom of the hole, Charlie stamps his feet in fury.

He immediately notices that the ground is soft.

Too soft.

It occurs to him now that it might collapse further at any moment, consigning him – possibly – to a muddy doom.

BANG!

Sure enough, the floor collapses, taking him twenty feet deeper into the hole.

Charlie is up to his waist in mud now and forty feet down.

He thinks he will never get out now.

He looks up at the space above him again, and the slippery walls, now even more vertiginous.

Eventually, after contemplating making the newly hazardous climb, he decides to stay where he is and hopes that someone will come and save him.

Even though he is essentially in the middle of nowhere.

(Basically his philosophy of life so far has been: 'If at first you don't succeed, give up.')

He tries to make a phone call for help.

He can't get a signal. After all, he's deep in a hole in the wilderness.

Minutes pass, then hours.

He shouts for help until his throat is hoarse.

No one responds.

He's getting cold and he's getting hungry.

Perhaps waiting for someone to come along isn't the optimal solution.

Also, he needs to get out and get to the insurance company.

But he still just waits, stumped, and does nothing.

After a period of marinating in self-pity and panic, and cursing the gods, the mining company, the local town council, the phone company and anyone else he can think of (Charlie always plays the victim), he finally spots one possible way out – he notices that the deeper hole has exposed a network of cables that he can use to haul himself upwards.

What are the cables?

Are they electrified?

Charlie thinks they very well might be.

He is tempted once again just to stay in the hole rather than risk death by trying to get out.

Apart from anything else, he can't see properly now his glasses have disappeared.

After all, it is a very limited life in the hole, but he is at least alive, and therefore 'safe'.

At least for the time being.

Sooner or later someone will probably come along.

It might take a day or two, but when he doesn't come home his wife will start searching and they will find the abandoned car and put two and two together. There are footprints on the ground that lead in this direction.

But he will lose the job he's hoping for. And even a free-and-easy company is not easily going to forgive him for not turning up at all, hole or no hole.

And his wife will probably leave him – even though it

wasn't his fault (except that if he'd filled the car with gas in the first place he wouldn't be in this pickle).

If no one comes along, he will have to spend the night in the dark with the worms, which he definitely doesn't like (though not as much as he doesn't like rattlesnakes).

Not a prospect he relishes, but it's safer than trying to get out.

All the same – the thought of his wife's anger at his hopelessness and lack of resourcefulness pushes him forward.

Reluctantly, he begins to scramble up the slippery sides of the hole again.

But the cables he uses to pull himself up *are* electrified, as he feared – and he receives a tremendous shock.

BANG!

He falls all the way back into the hole – twisting his ankle painfully on the way.

Jeopardy has increased once again.

He is now hungry and thirsty and severely weakened from all the effort he put into the climb last time. He is half blind and has suffered burns from the contact with the electrical cables.

He is in pain.

Charlie has a very low tolerance for pain.

He looks despairingly up at the crack of sky at the top of the hole.

He prays to God to get him out of this.

Then, something poking out of the muddy wall of the hole catches his eye.

The thing makes a horribly familiar sound.

It's a rattlesnake.

In fact, as Charlie watches in horror, he observes that it's a whole nest of rattlesnakes, writhing in and out of one another.

Just what he needs.

He has another choice to make.

Stay in the hole, spend the night in darkness, and quite possibly have a rattlesnake or two visit him.

Or he can make a break for it – somehow.

He can't do it.

He is defeated.

He slumps on the ground in total despair, closes his eyes and waits for the end of everything.

ooooo

This moment is not just *a* crisis.

It is *the* crisis. Or *worst point*.

It is the second major turning point in the story.

The word 'crisis' implies 'choice'. (It comes from the Greek word for 'decision'.)

A choice that Charlie is shortly going to make.

(The Chinese ideogram for 'crisis' has two meanings: 'danger' and 'opportunity'.)

In storytelling, all crises are invitations to enter a new world – to some extent. To break the boundaries of character.

*The* crisis, on the other hand, is one of the most profound tests of character in the plot.

In this case it is the moment when our hero, Charlie, can choose to change or choose not to change.

The crisis is the protagonist's opportunity to kill off their old self, to face their worst fears and emerge reborn.

Their choice is to deny change and return, humbled (or, perhaps, shamed), to their former self. Or confront their innermost fears, overcome them and be rewarded with a soul that is more complete, in balance, courageous and integrated.

ooooo

Out of the depths of his despair, Charlie looks up at the patch of blue sky at the top of the hole.

His eyes, without the correcting lens of his glasses, are able to focus properly on distance – something Charlie is almost never able to do.

The sky is so perfect and so blue.

A flock of richly coloured birds fly across the top of the hole.

An amazing cloud formation passes overhead.

So beautiful.

As a rule Charlie never looks at the sky or birds.

Not only has he got his problems with his eyesight, he thinks of himself as a pragmatist.

He doesn't see the point of birds and skies and, anyway, he's too busy inspecting the ground for holes.

But, on this occasion, forced to it by his adversity, he sees the sky and the birds and the clouds as if for the first time.

They seem to represent freedom, possibility, hope.

Inspired by this vision, Charlie gathers the last reserves of his courage.

He makes a key decision.

He decides to have another go at climbing out, despite his fears and trepidation – this time braving not only the impossible ascent and the electrical cables, but also the snakes.

## ACT THREE

Charlie's decision is the bridge into Act Three. And this *decision* is crucial – because it represents his transition from one sort of person into another.

(If he just stumbled upon a trampoline that happened to be buried at the bottom of the hole and bounced his way out, the story would have no *meaning*.)

The entire third act represents the story *climax* (also known as the *obligatory act*), during which a *final battle* is fought with the forces of darkness (in this case the hole and the snake – and Charlie's fear of the hole, of snakes and of risk generally).

(*Obligatory act* because, obviously, if Charlie just stayed in the hole, it wouldn't be much of a story.)

The word 'climax', according to Robert McKee, implies 'meaning', just as the word 'crisis' implies 'choice'.

The climax is the final *sequence of events* (not a single event) that carries maximum meaning in a story.

If the rest of the story up until this point is the flight of an arrow, then the climax is the target.

If the point of a joke is the punchline, then the point of a story is the climax.

The protagonist enters the last act with one concrete objective – to defeat the antagonist, to overcome their demons, to get home, to get the girl (or boy).

Or, in Charlie's case, to get out of the hole, get to the job interview, get the job and save his house and marriage.

So (inspired by his vision of the sky and the birds) he tries to climb out of the hole once again.

As he starts to make his way up, he discovers he possesses all sorts of qualities he *never knew he had* – resilience, courage, physical skill, willpower.

After many interesting slips, setbacks and near misses (which I can't be bothered to invent for this story), he makes it to the level where the snakes are.

Just beyond the snake nest is the top of the hole.

He hopes that the snakes are asleep, or slithering about on the surface – or something.

He is gingerly climbing past the nest when one particularly large rattler appears – level with his face.

Charlie does battle with the rattlesnake and defeats it in some appropriately ingenious way (which, once again, I can't be bothered to invent).

This is known as the *final battle* (or the *climactic moment*). It is lodged within the climax, or third act.

It's the moment when Luke Skywalker has to find the infinitesimally small target on the Death Star, or when Tom Cruise has to find and destroy the (remarkably similar) target at the climax of *Top Gun: Maverick*.

For Charlie it's finding a way to defeat the snake.

After nearly being bitten, poisoned or otherwise deprived of life and limb, Charlie makes mincemeat of that damn snake one way or another.

And thus makes it, at last, to the top and out onto the empty landscape.

He has confronted and overcome the things he fears most – snakes and holes – and he is still in time for his crucial meeting.

If he can just run fast enough.

Which means not staring at the ground for once in his life.

But this isn't the end of the story (although we are on the other side of the climactic moment).

We are now entering the *resolution* stage of the third-act climax.

As Charlie runs, he becomes aware that he has stopped looking at the ground.

He notices the colourful balloons and the drifting clouds and hears the birds sing.

Overcome by beauty and relief, he makes the interview just in time.

He walks into the insurance office, dirty and dishevelled (remember, he was previously convinced that it was appearances that mattered most), but supremely confident and entirely unselfconscious.

Despite his grubby demeanour, he wows the office manager with his new-found self-belief.

The manager gives him the job on the spot.

When he gets home his wife is thrilled and gives him a delighted hug and maybe even leads him to the bedroom.

On the way upstairs, he sees another worm in the kitchen, casually picks it up, examines it, then puts it gently down in the garden.

The story is thus resolved and reaches its conclusion.

What are the elements of the resolution?

There has been a *reversal* (cowardice into courage), a *reward* (the job, his wife) and a *rebirth* (Charlie is different, more complete).

In other stories, this reward may be a new-found power, or understanding. It may be a real prize, like the Holy Grail in Arthurian legend, or treasure. Or becoming a 'real boy' for Pinocchio. Dorothy gets to go home and discovers home is the most important thing.

This resolution, like the climax as a whole, has to come as a consequence of previous events and the cumulative choices the protagonist has made throughout the story.

ooooo

This is not a picture of how the world works.

It is a picture of how we would *like* it to work.

However, that is not to say it does not contain some important truths.

If you are dominated by your fear, you will end up stuck in a hole, albeit a metaphorical one, with snakes, albeit metaphorical ones, waiting to gobble you up.

You might call this – 'fear will destroy you' – the theme of the story.

ooooo

It's not much of a story – I know.

I've left gaps in it. (How does he defeat the snake? What are the ingenious methods he uses to make his way up the hole?) And frankly, it's not all that believable.

But I've certainly seen more implausible Hollywood movies.

The thing is, it's a *story*.

(Or, to be precise, a *plot*.)

My story of Charlie has stasis, an inciting incident, a goal (desire), rising jeopardy, a ticking clock, a worst point, a climax and a resolution.

It is governed by causality. It has a theme, albeit a fairly banal one. And each incident is there for a purpose.

It is populated with turning points, major and minor, difficult decisions, reversals and tests.

As it's in the early stages of drafting, I expect it to be pretty slight. And it is. But the basic mechanism is there.

If I can ever be bothered to go back and rewrite it twenty more times, it will be better.

Although I can't imagine it ending up as anything I would dare submit to a publisher.

It does have one particularly worrying flaw, though.

Being for the most part about only one character, there is very little dialogue, and therefore there is a massive gap in the potential for exploring human dynamics (which is what good writing is largely about).

It's very difficult to construct a story with only one character (although it can be done). Such a story is likely very focused on the interior, that is, reliant on internal narration.

Or, depending on how I write it, the story will be mostly exterior, that is, just 'things happening' and not much else.

There is little scope for interesting scenes between conflicted, warring personalities.

Other than the conflicted, warring personalities within Charlie.

But that's a problem I can, again, hopefully solve in later drafts.

At the moment I have simply got the problem of not enough happening generally. Or not enough happening that is meaningful.

The story needs some added complexity or occurrence.

Maybe I could get his phone working somehow to generate some new voices.

Or introduce a flashback or two. It's not 'live action', but it's at least action.

So: we have most of the key ingredients of a story in 'Charlie and the Hole'.

But we are still missing a very important moment (although it is potentially in there somewhere already, lost in all the other beats and reversals and pinch points).

This is the *mid-point* of the story.

# 5

## *'Charlie and the Hole': A Three-Act Story Incorporating Character and Plot – with a Mid-Point*

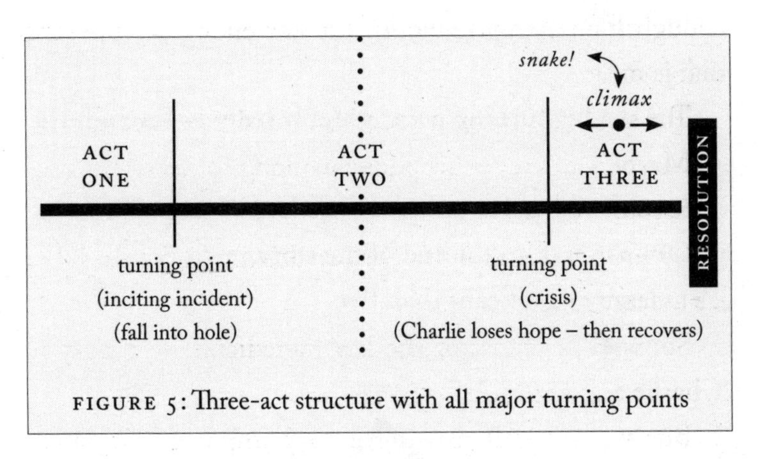


FIGURE 5: Three-act structure with all major turning points

In Figure 5 we can see the *mid-point* clearly marked, halfway through the second act (and halfway through the story as a whole).

The idea of the mid-point, although extensively explored by screenwriters, is often ignored by fiction writers and teachers. I have an extensive library of creative-writing books, spanning the last 100 years, yet barely any of them talk about the importance of the mid-point.

The long second act tends to drag unless you design the action very carefully. One common solution is to introduce subplots to get you through the 'swamps' of the second act.

But it's not much use for poor Charlie, since all the action is taking place through his eyes and there are no other characters in the second act. Although, of course, I could write more scenes back at the house with Charlotte and their daughter, Charlene (did I mention they had a daughter? Probably not – as I just made it up), from their points of view, thus introducing multiple protagonists.

The other (partial) solution to second-act 'drag' is the mid-point.

This is a big turning point roughly halfway through the action.

But the mid-point isn't just a method of propelling your narrator through to the end of the story.

It is more significant than that.

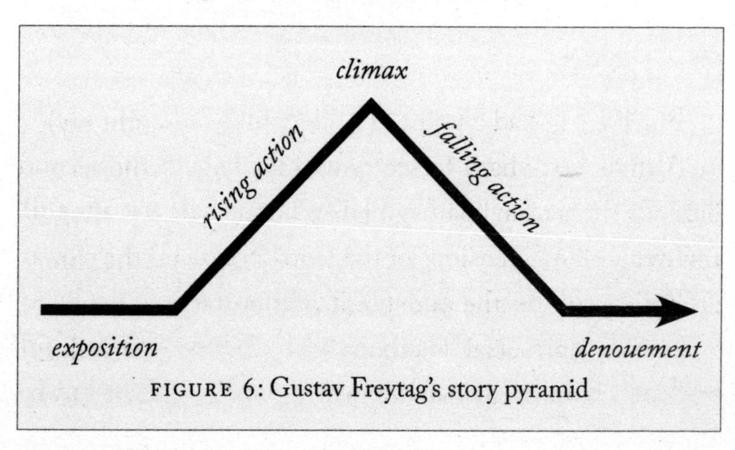


FIGURE 6: Gustav Freytag's story pyramid

It was Gustav Freytag, in his *Techniques of the Drama* (1863), who first suggested the importance of the mid-point.

Freytag thought a story plan should look like Figure 6, based on his study of Elizabethan and Jacobean drama, including the works of Shakespeare and Ben Jonson.

This pyramid is at first counter-intuitive – I had always envisioned plots looking much more like Figure 7, with tension rising until shortly before the end, then falling away:

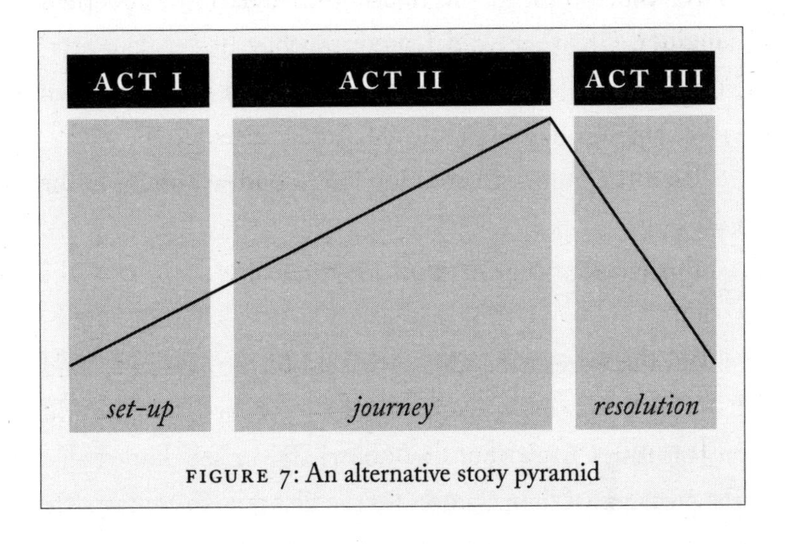


FIGURE 7: An alternative story pyramid

But Freytag had a point (a mid-point, you might say).

Although it's hard to see how the whole of the second half of a drama can be imagined as 'falling action' – after all, the steeply *rising* tensions of the worst point and the climax are still to come – the mid-point *is* important.

In fact, it's crucial – although, as already observed, for the novelist in particular the mid-point doesn't have to be exactly in the middle (which is where it can often be found in films and plays).

It is likely to be thereabouts, but the mid-point of the story, for novelists, is a conceptual moment or sequence, not a precise location in the narrative.

The mid-point represents a central pivot of the story.

It's not necessarily the most dramatic moment, but it is a moment of supreme significance.

The mid-point does not solve the protagonist's problem (created by the first big turning point).

It just gives them the first inkling of the solution, which will be grasped just before the end of the story, during the climax.

Here are some of the things that the mid-point *might* represent – or perhaps it might represent just one of them, or perhaps all of them at the same time.

1. *The point of no return.* Things have gone too far now for the protagonist to retreat and return to the life he has left behind.

2. *The mirror moment.* The dawning of a new truth for the protagonist, a flash of crucial knowledge or self-knowledge. The protagonist then chooses for the first time to confront the lesson they have to spend the rest of the story learning (and applying). It is the potential cure for, or key to, the problem raised at the inciting incident.

3. *Need* for the first time rises to the surface to supplant *want* (see Chapter 7).

4. The protagonist becomes proactive rather than reactive.

5. Something that is missing is found. Then the protagonist has to spend the rest of the story trying to 'take it home', or

apply it to their life. That which is found is usually a truth about themselves.

Regardless of which of these instances apply, the forces of antagonism are usually (further) aroused at the mid-point, and the jeopardy increases, putting the protagonist under greater and greater pressure.

For further explanation and examples of famous story mid-points, see Appendix 2.

ooooo

How can we apply the mid-point principle to my story of 'Charlie and the Hole'?

The trouble is, in going for a *very* simple set-up – 'man in hole' – I have, paradoxically, complicated matters.

The first complication, as I noted previously, is the lack of potential for dialogue.

The second is the lack of potential for varieties of jeopardy in the surroundings.

After all – Charlie is simply stuck in a hole. Alone.

He's not in a boardroom battle, or a fight against a serial killer, or on a boat with a psychopath, fighting a shark.

He's just a bit muddy and cold and frightened.

There's nothing very exciting about his surroundings.

They're just… well, a hole.

In order to design a meaningful mid-point, we have to go back to the beginning of the story and the establishment of Charlie's character and situation.

Let's say that he doesn't simply say goodbye to Charlene alone – Charlotte, his six-year-old daughter, is present in the scenario.

Instead of Charlie spotting a worm on the kitchen floor, let's substitute this scenario:

Little Charlotte walks up to Charlie just as he is about to leave.

She asks him to close his eyes and hold his hand out.

He does so, expecting a nice gift.

Instead, she hands him a wriggling worm. (Charlotte, who is quite naughty, knows about Charlie's phobias and knows full well that this prank will upset her father; it also represents her view of Charlie symbolically: he's a worm.)

Charlie, on cue, drops the worm and screams.

Upon which Charlene and Charlotte both burst into laughter.

Charlie feels humiliated.

As he leaves the house, he feels furious.

*What the hell?* he thinks. *What if my marriage does break up? So what? My wife is a ball-breaker who made me come back to this hellhole in the first place and my daughter is a brat.*

*I can always go and stay with my devoted but domineering and over-needy mother if the worst comes to the worst.*

*Now* we have set up the possibility of a proper mid-point.

ooooo

So once again, we join Charlie, stuck in his hole and stuck in Act Two.

He has been through the set-up and the inciting incident. He has an immediate problem to solve and a more long-term one (his passivity, which is possibly there as a result of having an overprotective mother).

At this stage he remains more or less reactive, or passive, rather than proactive.

There are worms down there, of course. Charlie really doesn't like worms.

Even so, rather than doing anything about his situation, as before he starts to cry and feel sorry for himself.

His mantra after leaving the house is now repeated.

*Screw the job.*

*Screw Charlene and screw Charlotte.*

*Who needs 'em?*

*I'll stay here.*

*I won't get the job, but someone will get me out eventually.*

*Yes, Charlene will probably leave me, but I can always go back to my mother's.*

THEN, there in the depths of the hole, tired and half asleep, at the mid-point of the second act (and the whole story), he half dreams, half remembers something his mother said to him when he was a child:

'You'll never amount to anything without me.'

He wakes with a start.

Maybe going back to his mother isn't such a good idea after all.

THEN he gets a ping on his phone.

Somehow it has found a signal!

He reaches urgently for the phone, but can't find it. Did it fall out of his pocket when he was tumbling down the walls of the hole?

Eventually he finds it, covered in mud.

He wipes the screen clean and checks the message, which he can just about make out without his spectacles.

Charlene has sent him a video.

It shows her and Charlotte saying sorry for being so rude to him, and saying they love him, and that they believe in him 100 per cent and that they know nothing will get in the way of his success at the job interview.

Another ping: one of the perennial complaining text messages he often gets from his mother:

'Charlie! Why haven't you called me?'

He angrily archives it and notices literally scores of similar messages: 'Where are you?' 'What are you doing?' 'Why aren't you here?'

All the same, despite his urgent dilemma, he wearily answers the text from his mother with one of his usual apologetic messages.

In doing so he inadvertently uses up the last reserves of his battery – before he has a chance to use the phone to call for help.

His unwarranted and irrational deference to his mother's demands has cost him his last chance to get out.

Now he stares hopelessly at the blank, black screen of his phone.

*In which he sees, with a shock, his tear-stained, pathetic reflection.*

It's his *mirror moment.*

Stressed, cold and afraid, he suddenly sees what he has become as a person.

Contemplating the video he's just watched, he realises how deeply he loves his wife and daughter. And how much they love him.

Spurred by this insight, he comes to a decision.

He *has* to get out of the hole, get the job and keep the house.

Not just for *himself*, but for Charlotte and Charlene.

As he stares at his now-dead phone, the battery used up by the texts to his mother, it also now occurs to him with the force of revelation that his mother is manipulative and domineering and has always held him back.

*Need* has replaced *want.*

At first, he just wanted to get out of the hole and get the job.

Now he has discovered his *need.*

Essentially, to grow up.

(Remember, in the first version of Charlie's story, what pushed him on towards making another attempt to get out of the hole was simply the thought of his wife's anger at his hopelessness and lack of resourcefulness. In other words, he was not really being proactive, but reactive, that is, he was driven by *fear* rather than insight and courage.)

*Now* he is proactive instead of passive.

He is acting positively, for the benefit of other people as well as himself.

He's going to endanger himself trying to get out, that's for sure.

But it's better than just rotting here and letting down his wife, his daughter and, finally, himself.

It's also better than staying a perpetual mummy's boy.

And so, as in the first version of this story (which lacks a mid-point), he battles with the snakes, runs to get to the job interview on time, gets the job, and order is restored.

But now we have a more fully developed three-dimensional protagonist, since Charlie has fundamentally changed and has a new understanding of who he is.

In the first version, the controlling idea is *overcoming fear*. In the second, it is still overcoming fear, but it also contains a greater measure of insight and character development for Charlie.

It gives the story a richer flavour – although the outcome is essentially the same.

Charlie is no longer dominated by his manipulative mother, and he recognises how much his daughter and wife love him, even though they might argue sometimes.

He has overcome his fear of crawling things (which perhaps only exists because he has hitherto been something of a 'crawling thing' himself).

He appreciates for the first time the wild, unpredictable beauty of nature – rather than trying always to reduce his life to a condition of perfect security by literally and metaphorically staring at the ground most of the time.

# 6

# *Plot (Part Two)*

## FIVE-ACT STRUCTURE:
## *How the Romans – and Shakespeare – thought about plot*

So far we have concentrated on the three-act structure in telling a story. But dramatic theory moved on after Aristotle.

The *five-act structure* is a dramatic model that stretches back to Roman times. (See Appendix 1.)

Towards the end of the first century BC, the Roman lyric poet Horace stated: 'Let no play be either shorter or longer than five acts.'

This paradigm was later adopted by Seneca, Shakespeare and Ben Jonson.

There is nothing particularly mysterious about the five-act structure.

All it does is elaborate the long second act into three parts.

In this model, however, there are three key stages lodged within the second act.

I will designate these three stages 'Act 2/5', 'Act 3/5' and 'Act 4/5'.

(In the five-act structure, the first and last act are the same as in the three-act structure.)

There are a number of ways of delineating these three key stages.

The scholar T. W. Baldwin, in his study *Shakespeare's Five-Act Structure* (1947), and Gustav Freytag (of 'Freytag's pyramid') both have definitions, but to me the most useful is that of Christopher Booker, author of *The Seven Basic Plots: Why We Tell Stories* (2004).

Booker identifies the first of these key stages lodged within the long second act as the *dream stage* of the narrative, the second as the *frustration stage* and the third as the *nightmare stage*.

During the dream stage, things go more or less according to plan for the hero.

Romeo and Juliet marry in secret.

Dorothy optimistically heads off to Oz on the Yellow Brick Road, having acquired her lovable companions.

Michael Corleone successfully protects his father against assassins.

Bridget Jones starts an affair with Daniel Cleaver and believes she has found love.

Philip Pirrip sets off to London to become a gentleman.

Macbeth becomes king.

In other words – the first *sub-goal* on the way to the *overarching goal* is achieved.

But then things start to go wrong.

The dream stage is immediately followed by the frustration stage (Act 3/5).

Here, it dawns on the protagonist that things are definitely going to get trickier before their final goal, the overarching goal (established by the end of Act One), can be achieved.

Estella proves elusive; Daniel Cleaver is untrustworthy; other gangs conspire to kill the Godfather.

The forces of antagonism gather – Malcolm, Macduff and Banquo, who are set in their role as antagonists to Macbeth by the murder of the king, defect and leave the court.

Juliet discovers she must be married to Paris; Romeo is banished for killing Tybalt; the Wicked Witch lets loose her first assaults on Dorothy.

The frustration stage straddles the mid-point.

On the other side of the mid-point, things continue to go wrong – only they get worse.

Events darken to the extent that the frustration stage mutates into the nightmare stage.

This is Act 4/5.

Macbeth murders Lady Macduff and her children, and is abandoned by all his former allies.

Juliet fakes death.

Pip learns, to his horror, that Estella is marrying Bentley Drummle and that the police are closing in on Magwitch, who will be hanged if he is caught.

The plot speeds up, trial heaping on trial.

The nightmare stage concludes with the crisis (which is the same as the crisis in the three-act drama), also known as the *worst point* or the 'darkest moment before the dawn'.

And then we are back to what we originally identified as the third act of the three-act structure: Act 5/5, the *climax* or *obligatory act*, comprising the *final battle* and the *resolution*.

ooooo

There is nothing to stop a novelist trying to impose a five-act structure on a novel, and often enough it comes naturally – but to try to pre-impose it too consciously can be restrictive and the writer may lose more than they gain.

Although I can locate the three-act structure readily enough in most classic novels, along with its key moments, the five-act drama is more slippery.

It feels more like a tool for dramatists and film-makers. For me, it seems that this structure is something that should emerge naturally, as it doubtless did for Dickens (*Great Expectations* has a classic five-act structure), rather than being consciously imposed on a text.

## MYTHIC STRUCTURE:
## *How Star Wars changed the way we think about stories*

Mythic structure is rooted not in the classical roots of story-telling, as the three- and five-act structures are – Aristotle,

Shakespeare, Freytag, and so on – but in Jungian psychoanalytic theory, in particular via the mythologist Joseph Campbell.

A promising young film producer, George Lucas, discovered Campbell's key work, *The Hero with a Thousand Faces*, in the 1970s. It posited that there was a universal shape to all stories, across all cultures.

He decided to apply the universal story principles he found in Campbell's book to his new film.

The result was *Star Wars*, the most successful movie franchise in history.

Doubtless Lucas would agree with Christopher Booker's statement:

> The real key to understanding stories lies in seeing how they are ultimately rooted in a level of the unconscious which is *collective to all humanity* [my italics]. [Chapter 31: 'Telling Us Who We Are']

In this model, also rooted in the works of psychoanalyst Carl Jung, story is the endless conflict between ego and id (or instinct).

This is what, in essence, the diagram in Figure 8 – taken from Christopher Vogler's *The Writer's Journey* (2007) – reflects.

You can immediately see a lot of parallels with classical theory.

The *ordinary world* is simply Act One, *stasis*.

It adds an extra element: the *refusal of the call*. This takes place after the first turning point, the *call to adventure*. The protagonist says no to the adventure, scared of what they might lose. Think of Luke Skywalker when he is originally given the chance to go in search of Princess Leia. His first reaction is to say no. Then his step-parents are murdered by Imperial stormtroopers and he changes his mind. Han Solo also refuses his first call, to pilot the *Millennium Falcon* with Luke on board.

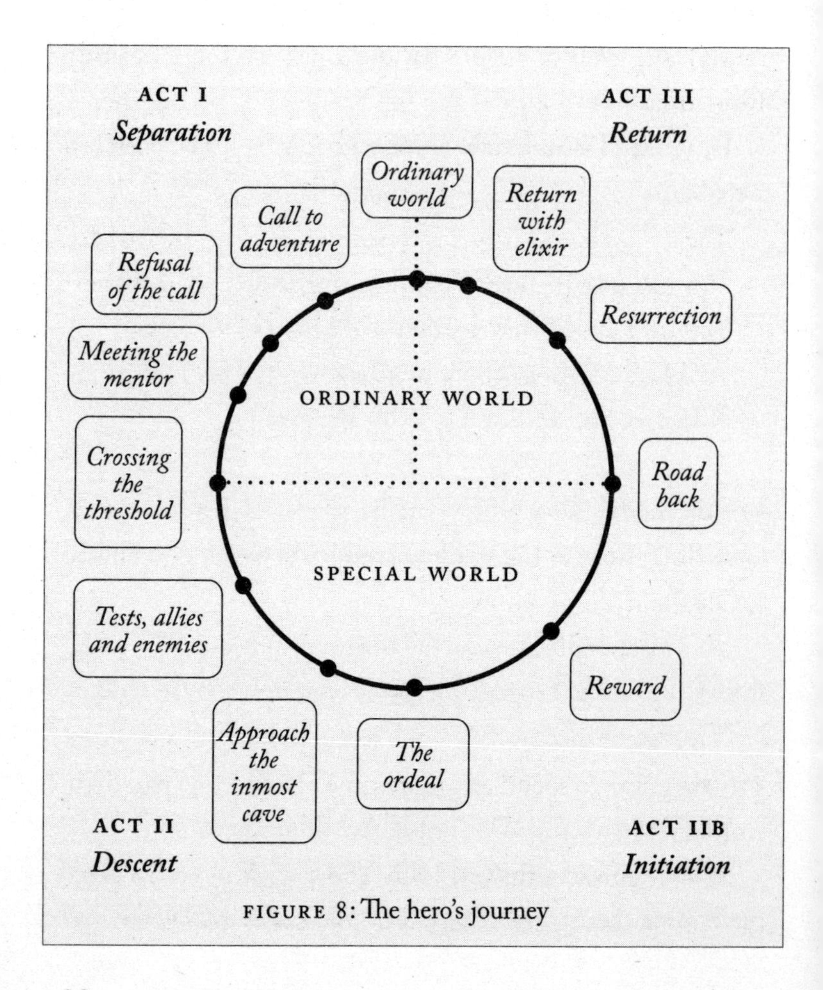


FIGURE 8: The hero's journey

*Crossing the threshold* is another major turning point, the moment the protagonist *makes the decision to get involved* in solving the problem that the first turning point ignited.

The mythic model adds a few other character elements to be thrown into the mix at the beginning of the story: the *mentor*, *allies* and *enemies*. For Luke, the mentor is Ben Kenobi; his allies are Chewbacca and Han Solo; his enemy is Darth Vader. For Dorothy in *The Wonderful Wizard of Oz* (1900), the mentor is Glinda, the allies are the Cowardly Lion, the Tin Woodman and the Scarecrow, and the enemy is the Wicked Witch of the West. (The Wizard himself is a weird amalgam of antagonist and ally.)

The *special world* is Act Two (or the void, or the woods).

Approach to the *innermost cave* and the *ordeal* are essentially both the mid-point and the crisis, respectively.

Act Three – well, who knows where Act Three is in the mythic paradigm?

It seems to skip straight to resolution – the *road back*, *reward*, *resurrection*, and so on. There's no third-act climax as such. The second half of the story in this model seems to be all about 'going home'.

ooooo

I'm not going to spend any more time plotting one paradigm onto another.

It just gets confusing. John Yorke makes a very good attempt at this in *Into the Woods*, if you want to read more.

But the *theory* behind the mythic model is pretty interesting. It goes as follows:

When humans became self-conscious beings they unleashed a storm of devils on the world that did not exist in the animal kingdom – envy, avarice, insanity, hatred, war, and much besides.

Each human being had a sense of their separate, individual existence. As Booker remarks, it makes no sense to think of an egocentric bee or elephant. An animal can have a level of consciousness, but its consciousness is entirely in sync with its unconscious self.

For humans it is different. We are *self-conscious* and we are therefore made up of two separate parts – the animal (unconscious) and the human (self-conscious).

Humans need to work to integrate the two parts of themselves in order to be balanced individuals.

We are divided in the way no other creature is, and our deepest need is for *internal unity* – to reconnect with our instinctive, universal, unconscious core.

The 'monster' in hero stories represents the ego, which has to be slain.

The ego-driven person becomes cut off from reality.

The egotist is driven ever further into unreality.

Epic stories (the main focus of mythic-structure theory) attempt to combat this pathological tendency.

These stories tell us about maturity, and about the death and rebirth involved in all the stages of life, from youth, to parenthood, to old age.

Mythic storytelling is about 'integrating the Shadow', a Jungian concept that suggests – to oversimplify – that there is darkness in the heart of every human being, and that if you do not acknowledge, that is, integrate, that dark part into your personality, then it has the potential to control you and possibly destroy you.

As I have said, this theory has some overlap in terms of content with classical structure but adds its own special elements.

Don't worry in the slightest if it doesn't make sense.

It *might* make sense if you throw your classical structure out of the window and try to redraw your mental map substantially, as well as read Christopher Booker's monumental (and fascinating) *The Seven Basic Plots*, Christopher Vogler's *The Writer's Journey* and Joseph Campbell's *The Hero with a Thousand Faces*.

But life is probably too short, unless you have ambitions to write an epic adventure along the lines of *Star Wars* or the *Odyssey* or Harry Potter or *The Lord of the Rings* (by no means an ambition to be disdained, but it may be beyond what most of us can hope for. A humble novel seems achievement enough).

ooooo

Incidentally, somewhere in the middle of my career as a novelist, I came across a copy of Vogler's *The Writer's Journey* and excitedly tried to construct a novel according to its precepts.

I failed.

The construction was far too constricting, obscure and complex.

Clearly, Hollywood film-makers find it useful. But I found it a mess – although I did use the trope of the *refusal of the call* once or twice in some of my later novels.

For John Yorke – to whom we shall come in a moment – mythic theory is no more than classical theory restated in different terms. 'Story structure,' says Yorke, 'is the perfect host for Jungian thought.'

## FRACTAL PATTERNS:
## *How every part of a story can reflect the whole*

I'm not going to spend too much time on this model of structure, brilliant though it is, because again I find it more relevant to screenwriters than novelists.

The 'fractal theory' (as I have christened it) was formulated by John Yorke in his book *Into the Woods*.

John is one of the most successful TV producers in Britain, and runs his own writing school.

John describes his own theory of structure, which is a further elaboration of classical three-act theory.

He suggests that narrative does not have three turning points, or four, or six – but fifteen, or more.

This is because, in his view, the shape of a single act exactly mimics the shape of the *story as a whole*.

So just as a story has three acts, so an act has three scenes – which in turn are composed of three 'beats'.

The endless refraction of narrative structure is going on within stories, acts, scenes and beats.

Turning points are everywhere – but they're not random. It's just a matter of how significant those turning points are.

One example John gives is the first act of the film *The King's Speech*.

> There are three very distinct stages: Bertie's terrible speech at Wembley; his wife's pursuit of a cure; and the first meeting between the future king and Logue... it has its own inciting incident (the speech); its own crisis (Bertie's choice whether or not to go); its own climax (the battle with Logue) and its very own clear midpoint – the moment where Elizabeth seeks out, in the darkened basement, her potential Australian cure. [Chapter 7: 'Acts']

And thus the climax of Act One is the inciting incident of Act Two. And so on.

Yorke sees this as a perfect harmony.

For him, in a properly constructed story, the final act is an exact mirror image of the first act.

Thus in *The Godfather* (1972), there are three parts of Act One: Michael is *honest* with Kay (his girlfriend); there is a celebration of life (the wedding); Michael's father is shot as a result of information provided by a traitor within the Corleone clan.

In Act Three: the traitor is revealed; there is an orgy of death; and Michael *lies* to Kay.

A precise reversal.

## SUBPLOTS:
## *What are they and why are they there?*

I don't have a great deal to say about subplots.

These second, third or fourth plots are usually less important than the main plot (although they can be equally so).

They also need to have a beginning, a middle and an end in order to constitute being a plot, albeit a secondary plot.

And they will ideally need to include at least one reasonably complex or three-dimensional character.

They will ideally feed into the theme – either supporting it or contradicting it.

(Think of the subplots in *King Lear*. They each echo or underline the main plot.)

If subplots don't connect up, they are no more than separate stories lodged within a novel, rather than an integral part of it.

And if they are made up of one- or two-dimensional characters and not connected to the theme or the main plot – what's the point of putting them in there?

They contradict the principle of unity.

And a proper fictional story – a *plot* – must have unity to be a plot at all.

The same applies to a subplot.

## CONCLUSION AND POSTSCRIPT TO CHAPTERS 1 AND 6:
### *The secret pattern of stories*

So now you have all the tools necessary to construct a plot – of some kind.

Is it of any use?

Possibly.

George Saunders likens the conscious imposition of plot at the beginning of a story to a nervous suitor going on a date with a set of index cards in his pocket.

These cards might read: '7:00 p.m. Inquire re childhood memories'; '7:15 p.m. Praise her outfit'; and so on.

This might be called over-planning.

With a plan we get to stop thinking. We can just execute.

But just as a conversation doesn't work like that, neither does a story.

ooooo

When I first became fascinated by story theory – in other words, *structure* – after attending an inspiring lecture by Robert McKee in 2016, I started to read everything I could find on the subject.

I quickly realised how complicated it was. As I delved deeper and deeper into the literature, what McKee expressed with beautiful clarity was suddenly in danger of disappearing under a swamp of definitions and counter-definitions and competing theories.

However, at its most fundamental, story theory can be of genuine use for the novelist, if handled with a light touch, flexibility and care.

It's best just to think of story structure not as a perfect, intricate map of plot, but as a few useful tricks that can be kept up your sleeve.

I could have just told you the 'tricks' – such as they are – but it is understanding *why* they work that makes them worth using.

Also, it would be a very short book comprising these simple sentences:

'Try to have a beginning, a middle and an ending.'

'Have plenty of turning points that engage the reader.'

'Oh, and it's quite useful to put a big moment in the middle.'

Or, to restate Peggy Ramsay – and to render it an even shorter book:

'It's just two or three little surprises followed every now and then by a bigger surprise.'

ooooo

Just in case this secret pattern of stories is all in my imagination – after all, it's impossible to *prove*; maybe this whole story structure is a con thought up by story teachers to justify their fees – I have examined ten well-known novels in order to locate the structure that underlies them. You can find those analyses in Appendix 3.

But I suggest you put your curiosity on hold for the time being – because the analyses only make full sense once you have knowledge of the second strand of the magic helix of storytelling: character.

# 7

# *Character (Part Two)*

## CONTRADICTIONS:
## *Desire, need, the divided self and the clash of opposites*

We concluded the first part of our examination of character by pointing out the various dimensions of a fictional character – one, two and three.

Now we are going to look at some of the other aspects of the human character and how they might play out in a story.

### *Desire*

Charlie Kaufman, in a speech to BAFTA in 2011:

> Every single moment, every single person wants something. Often many things, often conflicting things. Understand this about your characters and yourself.

Robert Olen Butler, in *From Where You Dream* (2006):

> We yearn. We are the yearning creatures of this planet. There are superficial yearnings, and there are truly deep ones always pulsing beneath, but every second we yearn for *something*. And fiction, inescapably, is the art form of human yearning. [Chapter 3: 'Yearning']

*We all want something.*

We can pretend we don't want anything, but if we didn't we wouldn't be human. In fact we would barely be alive at all. Even a plant wants something, even if it's only water and sunlight.

Most major characters in a story want something, but the protagonist in particular almost always has a desire to fulfil (or acquires one quite quickly) and will be proactive – sooner or later – in trying to achieve it.

It is usually, though not necessarily, the desire of the central character which drives the story.

Lizzy Bennet does not start *Pride and Prejudice* (1813) – a multi-protagonist story – with a particular desire for anything.

Neither does the turning point of Bingley's arrival at Netherfield spark one within her.

It is her *mother's* passionate desire – to see her daughters married – that drives the narrative, along with, later, Darcy's desire for Lizzy.

ooooo

This desire of a key character cannot be too general – like 'to be happy' or 'to find love'.

It has to be the concrete goal that the protagonist thinks will achieve those more general ends.

To be king. To get out of the hole. To get the girl back. To get rich. To eliminate a rival. To get the daughters married off.

As David Mamet puts it in *Three Uses of the Knife*:

> In the perfect play we find nothing extraneous to his or her single desire. Every incident either impedes or aids the hero/heroine in the quest for the single goal. [Chapter 1: 'The Wind-Chill Factor']

There are apparent exceptions to this. There are *always* exceptions to everything when it comes to writing, but they are usually only apparent.

Macon Leary, in Anne Tyler's *The Accidental Tourist* (1985), having been broken by the murder of his son, seems to want nothing at all, and to be entirely passive. He just wants to stay numb, which is the death of his soul. But what he really wants is… to want something.

Blanche DuBois in *A Streetcar Named Desire* (1947) seems mainly passive. But what she wants is to escape reality – a desire she finally achieves when she goes insane.

Nick Carraway is the passive narrator of *The Great Gatsby* (1925) – but he isn't the protagonist. He simply acts as witness to the real protagonist – Jay Gatsby, whose obsessive desire for Daisy drives the whole book.

There are doubtless other exceptions. Perhaps some of them even real, rather than apparent, exceptions, and perhaps such exceptions can even act as the engine for good stories.

All I can say is that, as a writing mentor who is constantly reading individual manuscripts from would-be writers, one of the most common flaws I experience is that the central character is passive throughout. Or for far too long. They don't desire anything in particular, they are just knocked about like a skittle by circumstance.

This usually makes for dull reading, because those characters are missing the most essential part of what it is to be human – desire.

Furthermore, lacking that desire, there is nothing for the storyteller to hang the action on, so the narrative tends to end up meandering.

The word 'drama' means 'a thing *done*' – not something happening *to you.*

At the beginning of any drama, the central questions I usually pose of my protagonist are: 'What do you want? How are you going to try to get it? And what stands in your way?'

This desire is known as the *superobjective* or *overarching goal.*

It represents the spine of the story, the formula that drives the plot forward.

Either the character is moving closer, or further away, from their goal.

Characters may not know their own desires (although they usually do) – but the *writer* has to.

The audience has to have a sense of the protagonist's desire, or they are unlikely to be interested in the outcome.

Desire doesn't just govern the story – arguably it should appear in each scene.

What does a character want when they go into a scene? What obstructs them?

In other words, what is their motivation?

As the playwright Leo Butler remarks:

> You'll have a much better time writing if you let at least one of your characters enter the scene with a motivation.

Charlie wants to get out of the hole. Boy wants to get girl back.

That's drama at its simplest.

If Charlie is perfectly happy in the hole, or the boy is fine with the girl leaving him, there is no drama because there is no desire.

A desire can also be thought of as a *want.*

I *want* the girl back, I *want* to get out of the hole.

However, there is another drive, related to desire or want, that lies under the surface of a rounded character.

This (often contradictory) drive is *need.*

*Need: 'You can't always get what you want.*
*But if you try sometime...'*

The film director Oliver Stone says that one should always ask what the character *needs* from the other character(s). Not wants, *needs.*

The fully formed protagonist often has a need as well as a desire.

Their *wants* are conscious desires they mistakenly believe will make them feel complete and calm the conflict within them.

But it is the underlying unconscious *need* that requires addressing, and this is often the core of the drama.

The story theorist Vladimir Propp called this need the 'lack' – which implies that something is missing in the protagonist which needs to be gained (or regained).

Only once this lack is rectified will the character become complete.

ooooo

We all hide behind masks.

We all hide behind masks. A character's mask can be thought of as a protective device against a repressed inner conflict.

People create a persona that makes them feel safe.

Need exists because the conscious mind often does not know what it lacks, since it often acts simply as the PR department of the unconscious mind.

Much of what we think – and think we want – is simply rationalisation.

Good fictional narratives set out to test and expose those rationalisations within a character.

What all characters *really* seek is not to become king or win the lottery – but to become whole.

But the key to becoming whole is often hidden from them.

The idea of the need or lack is closely related to the classical-Greek dramatic concept of *hamartia*, or 'flaw'.

Philip Pirrip wants to be a gentleman so he can fulfil his desire of winning Estella's heart.

But in the process he develops a flaw – spiritual pride.

It is this flaw that he needs to overcome before he can feel complete.

The flaw is not quite the same as the need.

The need is the *answer* to the flaw, and often the opposite to it.

For Philip Pirrip, as for King Lear, the flaw is pride, and the need is humility.

In his book *The Science of Storytelling*, Will Storr calls this element of character-building the 'sacred flaw'.

> We're looking for a specific kind of flaw – one that our character has formed a core part of their identity around and that has the potential to do them damage.
>
> A few years ago, I was lucky enough to interview the famous psychologist Professor Jonathan Haidt. He told me something I've never forgotten: 'Follow the sacredness. Find out what people believe to be sacred, and when you look around there you will find rampant irrationality.'
>
> Rampant irrationality! This is exactly what we should be hunting in our characters. In order to locate the thing they're irrational about, we need to ask what

> they make sacred. The things we make sacred are, to a great extent, the things that come to define us. This, I believe, is the secret of unlocking the truth of a character. When other people think of us – when they're asked what we're 'like' – our sacred belief will probably be the first thing that pops into their minds...
>
> A fictional character's 'sacred flaw', then, is the broken part of them that they've made sacred. [Appendix: 'The Sacred Flaw Approach']

Or, to put it another way: 'A character's flaw is merely knowledge not yet learned' (John Yorke, *Into the Woods*).

ooooo

There is another, more modern way of looking at the subject, rooted in psychoanalysis.

That is, to view the flaw as a 'wound' – the wound that caused the flaw that led to the need (so to speak).

Here Charlie Kaufman, in his BAFTA speech, reveals his own *hamartia*:

> I spend most of my time trying to get you to like me... It is an ancient pattern of time usage for me... This pattern of time usage paints over an ancient wound, and paints it with bright colours. It's a sleight of hand, a distraction, so to attempt to change the pattern let me expose the wound. I now step into this area blindly,

> I do not know what the wound is, I do know that it is old. I do know that it is a hole in my being. I do know it is tender. I do believe that it is unknowable, or at least unable to be articulable.
>
> I do believe you have a wound too. I do believe it is both specific to you and common to everyone. I do believe it is the thing about you that must be hidden and protected, it is the thing that must be tap-danced over five shows a day, it is the thing that won't be interesting to other people if revealed. It is the thing that makes you weak and pathetic. It is the thing that truly, truly, truly makes loving you impossible. It is your secret, even from yourself. But it is the thing that wants to live.
>
> It is the thing from which your art, your painting, your dance, your composition, your philosophical treatise, your screenplay is born.

This expresses beautifully how much of great storytelling rests on the revelation of the flaw, the need, the wound, that we all keep hidden within ourselves – as much for the writer or the reader as for the fictional character.

Having established in the first act the goal of the protagonist, we will eventually learn about their flaw – or at least we will be given clues to it, as it reveals itself during the narrative.

This flaw, incidentally, can also, and often does, act as the antagonist of the story. (Antagonists do not have to be external, as they are in most detective and adventure stories.)

Flaws come in many varieties. The important thing is that during the drama the protagonist uncovers it and starts to struggle with it.

To summarise:

The *want* is more superficial, more ego-driven than the *need*.

The flaw, need, lack or wound, being unconscious, needs to be brought to the surface and confronted during the course of the narrative in order for the character to become properly integrated.

'A neurosis is a secret you don't know you're keeping,' remarked the drama critic Kenneth Tynan.

The thing about the *persona* is that people don't know they have one. It's not that they are consciously 'putting on an act'.

This lack of self-knowledge is compounded and maintained by the fact that the central character will often dress up their flaw as a virtue.

Louise in Ridley Scott's film *Thelma and Louise* is a control freak masquerading (to herself) as someone tough and resilient, whereas in fact she has lost touch with her ability to feel. Thelma thinks her childlike nature is lovable, whereas it is in fact dangerously naive.

What Pip experiences as growing sophistication and worldliness is actually the accretion of blind arrogance and romantic obsession.

The drama therefore represents a road map of change – one that charts a growing awareness of the protagonist's flaws and their gradual acceptance and therefore integration of those flaws.

ooooo

The collision between *need* and *want* often becomes most apparent at the mid-point of the story.

Here, a clue is uncovered as to the flaw within the character (not necessarily a *solution* – just a *clue*).

For examples, see Appendix 4.

In each case, the protagonist has to be taken to an extreme moment in their life to start facing up to their need.

In each case, they are suffering and full of doubt and uncertainty.

As Will Storr points out in *The Science of Storytelling*:

> It takes overwhelming evidence to convince us that 'reality' is wrong. When we finally realise something's up, breaking these beliefs apart means breaking ourselves apart.

Storr also states:

> Stories such as this are like life itself, a constant conversation between conscious and subconscious, text and subtext. [Chapter 3: 'The Dramatic Question']

This fundamental conflict – conscious versus subconscious – is, however, only one of the many contradictions that human beings experience.

## *The divided self*

Humans are not only divided between their conscious and unconscious minds.

They are divided along many other axes – for example, their need to be social beings, acting for the collective good, while pushing forward their more selfish, individual aims.

As Storr puts it:

> Humans are driven to connect and dominate... It's the conflict at the heart of the human condition and the stories we tell about it. [Chapter 3: 'The Dramatic Question']

To put it another way, humans are built to be both selfish and unselfish and can be pulled in either direction at any time.

It makes people unpredictable, which is what fascinates us about character.

As the author and story theorist David Corbett puts it in *The Art of Character*:

> [Contradictions] express a seeming paradox of human nature: that people do one thing and exactly the opposite; they're this, but they're also that. [Chapter 9: 'The Paradox of This but That: Contradictions']

This contradiction is eternal. As St Paul noted many centuries ago:

> For what I do is not the good I want to do; no, the evil I do not want to do – this I keep on doing. [Romans 7:19]

So how can we build a convincing character out of someone who must be recognisably the person they are (Aristotle's repeated action) as well as their unpredictable part?

It is impossible to be precise about the answer, because it goes again to the heart of the question: 'What is a person?'

It is the writer's job to explore that question, not answer it.

Here's David Corbett again, writing in the *New York Times* in 2013, on contradiction:

> Simply stated, a contradiction is something about a person that piques our interest because it betrays what we expect, given what else we know or observe about him.
>
> We see the two polarities, the contrasting yin and yang of the behaviour, and automatically wonder at the invisible domain that lies between.
>
> Contradictions are also intrinsically interesting. Our perceptions are instinctively geared toward seeking out what doesn't fit. This is evolutionarily adaptive: It alerts us to threats. That unexpected sound we hear could simply be the wind in the grass – or a predator approaching. Your normally placid neighbour's bout of cursing could be nothing – or something you ignore at your peril. The underlying message of every contradiction is: Pay attention.

Other contradictions are based on our need to fulfil widely different social roles, he continues:

> In 'Rameau's Nephew', Denis Diderot proposed that each of us is obliged to assume multiple personas to fulfill the seemingly endless number of obligations demanded of us. We conduct ourselves appropriately in a variety of different social situations: the dinner table, the office, the chapel, the bedroom. We feel differing degrees of freedom to 'be ourselves' in each of these environments, depending on who else is present, our relationship with them, our status. But most people effortlessly navigate such diverse circumstances daily. We are, each of us, masters of contradiction.

Another novelist, Junot Díaz, has this to say about contradictions:

> [As a writer] you need to have a strong sense of how the average person carries their contradictions – for that is what all of us humans have and what often defines our characters – their contradictions.
>
> You need to study the contradictions of people around you and think about how certain kinds of contradictions could lead certain kinds of characters into certain kinds of trouble. All of this will help in creating nuanced characters.

> Just always remember the Golden Rule – which is not that you want characters that you can like or dislike – but characters whom we get to understand, a process that allows us to understand parts of ourselves.

The principle of contradictions may suggest that your character can behave any way the writer feels without sacrificing plausibility.

However, contradictions are *not* random.

As McKee put it in a lecture: 'Character dimensions are *consistent contradictions*. Not a nice guy who on one occasion kicks a dog.'

### *The clash of opposites*

The role of opposites is a well-explored theme in story theory, although it is frequently over-explained to the point where it starts to become incomprehensible.

This is partly because it has become entangled with Jungian psychological theory – most particularly as a result of Joseph Campbell's *The Hero with a Thousand Faces* and Christopher Booker's epic *The Seven Basic Plots*.

Central to Booker's view is that many narratives are animated by the collision of opposites.

This could be the collision of Pip and Abel Magwitch in *Great Expectations*, or Lizzy Bennet and Mr Darcy in *Pride and Prejudice*. It could also refer to Thelma and Louise, or any number of superheroes and their adversaries.

The idea is that the externalised *antagonist* (which is not always the same as an enemy) acts as an agent to draw out the 'dark side' of their opposite – the 'goodie' – and thus bring that dark side into daylight, thereby neutralising it, or at least rendering it more subject to control.

Out of these opposites is created a whole.

Being rooted in Jungian theory, it isn't that simple.

For a start, the dark side (what Jungians call 'the Shadow') represented by the antagonist is often not dark at all.

Abel Magwitch is humble and selfless, which makes Pip aware of his own lack of humility and selflessness. But he is Pip's antagonist (or one of them).

He is only a 'dark side' or Shadow from the point of view of Pip.

Charlie Allnut draws out the instinctive side of the more repressed Rose in the John Huston film *The African Queen* (1951), while she civilises and tames him.

Charlie and Rose each *see* the other as 'dark', as their Shadow, but they are in fact 'light'.

The Shadow, according to the Jungians, having been animated, responds when faced with its opposite.

Hamlet could be said to 'incorporate' his Uncle Claudius's ruthlessness in sending Rosencrantz and Guildenstern to their deaths, and resolving finally to kill off Claudius.

With dual protagonists – especially in 'buddy' movies – we see a similar process take place.

At the start of *Thelma and Louise*, Thelma is childish and naive and easily led, while Louise is tough and cynical.

By the end of the film, Louise has discovered her more tender, natural self, and Thelma has become decisive and wilful.

(There is a scene where Ridley Scott spells this out for us when they are about to set off on their road trip. Thelma puts on Louise's hat, snatches her cigarette, looks pointedly in the mirror and says playfully, 'Look, I'm Louise!' It's a foreshadowing – a mirror image – of what is to come.)

So opposites can swap roles, they can take on one another's vices or virtues, although the 'vice' can be a virtue and virtue a vice.

In order to become a mob boss Michael Corleone has, like Hamlet, to take on the 'virtue' of ruthlessness to become complete.

In *The Writer's Journey*, Christopher Vogler (one of the central figures of 'mythic' theory) makes this distinction between the 'antagonist 'and the 'enemy'. He observes:

> Shadows can be all the things we don't like about ourselves, all the dark secrets we can't admit, even to ourselves... The Shadow can also shelter positive qualities that are in hiding or that we have rejected for some reason.
>
> The negative face of the Shadow in stories is projected onto characters called villains, antagonists, or enemies. Villains and enemies are usually dedicated to the death, destruction, or defeat of the hero. Antagonists may not be quite so hostile – they may be Allies who are after the same goal but who disagree with the hero's tactics. ['Shadow']

So Thelma and Louise are mutual antagonists.

But they are not enemies.

The patriarchy is the enemy.

ooooo

One can play with this idea endlessly, and it contains much that is fruitful.

For me, however, it's a little overcomplicated and it's better simply to call it 'learning from someone different from you'.

People *learn*, for good or ill, from their antagonists, who are often but not always their opposites (and often, but not always, their enemies).

The thing to hold on to when it comes to opposites is simply the recognition that a lot of stories rely on this opposition.

John Yorke would say it was another example of 'thesis, antithesis, synthesis', the learning process made implicit.

You start off in one condition (thesis); you are brought face to face with your antagonist (antithesis); and then you learn something from them (synthesis).

This 'learning' again is Janus-faced.

Arthur Fleck in *Joker* (2019) learns from a brutal, chaotic society to be cruel and destructive and to fall in love with chaos.

In this, he represents the 'dark side' of Batman, who represents law and order.

For a Jungian, the Joker represents the repressed side of Batman's own secret cruelty and love of power and desire for mayhem.

But one doesn't have to be a Jungian simply to acknowledge that there are opposites in play.

One doesn't have to believe that Batman and the Joker are each repressing reflecting sides of one another to understand that coming into collision with your opposite is the ultimate challenge, and that such a challenge has potential for both drama and learning, on either side.

And you don't have to believe that you (or your character) is 'repressing' something in order to put two forces in opposition and watch the sparks fly – what John Yorke calls 'the dance of opposites'.

So Wiesler, the cold-hearted protagonist in Florian Henckel von Donnersmarck's film *The Lives of Others* (2006), assimilates his opposite – empathy – as a result of secretly bugging his subjects as part of his operations as a member of the Stasi.

But those he observes learn nothing from him in return. Except perhaps that their 'enemy' is, after all, human.

Bridget Jones learns nothing from her enemy, Daniel Cleaver, or, for that matter, from her antagonist, Mark Darcy. And they don't seem to learn anything from her (although Mark Darcy does loosen up a bit).

But these are still effective oppositions.

The Jungian view is that, in John Yorke's words, 'the assimilation of darkness is crucial to growth.'

Which is to say, what or who the character hates or fears will, if acknowledged and accepted, make them whole.

The Shadow can be disempowered – though not entirely

neutered – by our assimilating, that is, accepting on a deep level, the buried, denied part of ourselves.

In order to do so, we have to bring it to light, and that, for Jungians, is what many stories are about – the bringing to light of the part of ourselves that we have denied.

The Shadow can be disempowered like a vampire by being brought to light – the light of consciousness.

ooooo

Perhaps the Jungians are right.

Perhaps we all need to get in touch with our dark, life-denying and aggressive forces and bring them into the light.

But you don't *have* to believe, or understand, that principle in order to write good oppositional characters.

It's enough to acknowledge that people with fundamental differences can learn from each other when they come powerfully enough into opposition.

And it is that simple principle – rather than the complexities of psychoanalytic theory – which lies at the heart of storytelling.

## CHOICE AND ACTION:
*The heart of character*

If the question at the heart of storytelling is 'who *is* this person?', then the answer is revealed mostly by *the choices that person makes.*

Humans are compelled by stories which have the theme of choice at their heart, because we have to make countless choices every day.

This is our freedom as human beings – but it comes at the price of the possibility of making mistakes and the prospect of regret.

Who are we?

Perhaps we don't start to find out until we have to make a difficult choice.

We can say, and think, that we are one thing, but, under the pressure of life, find out we are something – someone – else entirely.

I imagine that very few of the people who were complicit in the crimes committed during the period of Nazi rule in Germany had any comprehension of what they were capable of prior to the arrival of the regime.

Many would doubtless have insisted that they would never have cooperated in such a project.

But when the time came, under pressure of fear for their own safety, or of the consequences of standing out from the crowd, many made the decision to fall in line with a murderous regime – and perhaps made subsequent choices that they never imagined they could make.

Perhaps they even enjoyed the terrible outcome of those choices.

They found out that they were not who they thought they were.

Such choices ripple out endlessly, as is demonstrated in

William Styron's *Sophie's Choice* (1979), a book entirely driven by a single decision, and the terrible question: 'What would you do if you were forced to choose between the death of both of your children or saving only one of them?'

Such a choice is faced by Sophie. It is imposed on her by a sadistic concentration-camp guard. How can she live with such a choice?

And incidentally, it suggests another question not addressed by the book: would the camp guard have believed that he was capable of such an action ten years previously?

Almost certainly not.

But *his* choice – to torment an already tormented mother – revealed who he really was, or, at least, what he was capable of.

Such a story takes to an extreme the questions we all have to face.

How do we live with our choices?

And what do our choices tell us about who we are?

Choices are not choices until they become actions.

Sophie might have said up until that point that she would have chosen one child rather than the other.

Perhaps when the circumstance occurred she chose a different child to the one she imagined was her favourite, thus revealing her true feelings to herself.

The action crystallises the hypothetical choice into irrevocable reality.

Which is why we are compelled by the choices that lead to actions.

The greater the pressure, the deeper and truer the choice.

'Faced with extreme stress, some will laugh, some will cry, some will intellectualise, others will punish others,' said McKee.

And they will often not know which – until the moment of choice arrives.

One of the most brilliant depictions of a moment of choice in cinema is that in *The Godfather* when Michael Corleone is faced with the action of shooting in cold blood a corrupt police chief and a mob boss.

Coppola lets the camera play on Pacino's eyes, and we can see his inner struggle. Which is not merely 'Can I do this?' but 'Who am I if I do this?'

His whole future as a human being is contained within that single moment.

The sound of a passing train screeching underlines his inner agony.

And then he takes out his gun and shoots the police chief and the mob boss both – thus setting into train the death of his own soul and conscience.

This moment, not coincidentally, is the mid-point of the film.

## EMPATHY:
## *Must your characters be 'likeable'?*

Perhaps the most baffling remark made by my otherwise wonderful book editor when presented with one of my (failed) attempts to secure a book deal was 'I don't like the characters'.

To which I might have responded (I didn't) by referring her to Claire Messud when she was asked, in a 2013 interview for *Publishers Weekly*, about a supposedly unlikeable character in one of her novels, and whether the author would like to be friends with that character.

> For heaven's sake, what kind of question is that? Would you want to be friends with Humbert Humbert? Would you want to be friends with Mickey Sabbath? Saleem Sinai? Hamlet? Krapp? Oedipus? Oscar Wao? Antigone? Raskolnikov? Any of the characters in *The Corrections*? Any of the characters in *Infinite Jest*? Any of the characters in anything Pynchon has ever written? Or Martin Amis? Or Orhan Pamuk? Or Alice Munro, for that matter? If you're reading to find friends, you're in deep trouble. We read to find life, in all its possibilities. The relevant question isn't 'is this a potential friend for me?' but 'is this character alive?'

There are plenty of editors and agents who do not agree with Messud.

The 'likeability' of characters is often considered paramount for many book publishers.

I think this is a limited view, and results from a confusion between the terms 'sympathy' and 'empathy'.

Sympathy, as Robert McKee remarks, is optional, while empathy is absolute.

This is another way of saying, as McKee remarked in a lecture:

> A character must be empathetic. 'Empathetic' means 'like me'. Shared humanity. It's not the same as sympathy. It's the observation 'that character is a person like me'. The audience is rooting for themselves.

This is why we can care about the monstrous Macbeth.

Because although he does terrible things he is tortured by them and driven by a combination of his ambition, his equally monstrous wife and the malevolent Wyrd Sisters.

In other words, we do not have to 'like' a protagonist, but to *identify* with them.

As for antagonists, modern villains are rarely like Bill Sykes in *Oliver Twist* (1838): unremittingly animal, brutal and cruel.

Modern villains often have style, power, wit, charisma, intelligence.

We may not root for Hannibal Lecter, but we recognise that he is clever, charismatic – cool, even.

As for the protagonist, they may not have to be likeable, but you have to understand where they are coming from, and perhaps what led them to be the way they are.

You have to care about them to some extent, even if they are terrible.

This is empathy rather than sympathy.

This is recognising something of yourself in the character.

Blake Snyder's screenwriting book *Save the Cat* (2005) is so called because it references the moment early on in any hero film in which the protagonist 'saves the cat' (or baby, or helpless old lady) so that they can engage our sympathy.

But this is a somewhat blunt tool, because likeability is not the key to a good narrative.

Every single character in the TV series *Succession* is deeply dislikeable. This doesn't stop it being compelling viewing, because we sense that each one of the children of the monstrous Logan Roy is damaged and desperately seeking his approval.

Having said all that, it probably won't do you any harm at all, commercially speaking, to create a lead character that the reader can like, root for and feel on the side of.

Nasty protagonists, although they are fascinating, can be a harder sell (although it is disturbing how the film *Downfall* (2004) makes us empathise with Adolf Hitler himself – at least in the first part of the film).

But a novel without at least some nasty characters would be rather thin gruel.

And when the nasty and nice characters are combined into one person – as they are, say, in Elizabeth Strout's *Olive Kitteridge* – we are compelled.

What makes you care about a character – even if you don't necessarily 'like' them?

The same thing that makes you care about a person.

First, you have to know them.

It helps if they are characters we like or wish we were like, but it's not mandatory.

Secondly, they have to have vulnerabilities.

Thirdly, they have to be in some kind of *jeopardy* so you can worry about what happens to them. (Aristotle called for the writer to aim to generate 'pity and fear' for the main character.)

Fourthly, they have to have difficult choices to make in which the stakes are high.

And they have to *want* something.

We have already talked about desire. Desire in a character makes them resemble us, because we all desire something.

Also, the character will usually think of themselves as the underdog, just as we always see ourselves as the underdog.

We love an underdog – which is why everyone gets so excited when a no-hoper team wins the Premier League.

Because it suggests that even a loser like you or me can come back from nowhere and achieve something astonishing.

## *Some final thoughts on character*

- You should polarise the cast of characters. Each main character should have different attitudes from the rest towards *everything*. No two characters should react the same. All characters must have their own point of view.

- 'Drama is a conversation between characters who are all arguably in the right' – David Mamet.

  This is one of the best pieces of advice on character I have come across. Any viewer of Mamet's films or plays will be conscious of the ground constantly shifting beneath them, as their sympathies shift from place to place.

- Get the *right name*.

  It sounds trivial, but it isn't. Think of Charles Ryder and Sebastian Flyte in *Brideshead Revisited* (1945). One rides, the other flies – then falls.

  Would *The Hunger Games* (2008) be the same if 'Katniss Everdeen' was 'Doris Splott'?

  Names are like little poems (like book titles).

  Somehow they have to fit the character.

- Character development is slow, organic. Don't expect it to happen right away.

  The characters in early drafts of my novels are always cardboard cut-outs. They don't really develop believable characteristics until I've lived with them for a while. You *discover* the person rather than just 'make them up'.

  Elizabeth Bowen:

> One cannot 'make' characters, only marionettes. The manipulated movement of the marionette is not the 'action' necessary for plot. Characterless action is not action at all, in the plot sense. It is

> the indivisibility of the act from the actor, and the inevitability of *that* act on the part of *that* actor, that gives action verisimilitude. Without that, action is without force or reason. Forceless, reasonless action disrupts plot. The term 'creation of character' (or characters) is misleading. Characters pre-exist. They are *found*. They reveal themselves slowly to the novelist's perception – as might fellow travellers seated opposite one in a very dimly lit railway carriage. The novelist's perceptions of his characters take place *in the course of the actual writing of the novel.*

- If you know a character, you care about them. If someone comes in on the first page and shoots someone else, you are unlikely to be repelled by the killer or concerned about the victim.
- You have to know characters far better than they know themselves. Better than a psychiatrist. You've got to get past their lies and rationalisations... until you get to what they *really* want (need).
- Always check the character's motivation – *why* does a character want what they want?
- Don't let them do something unless it's believable, at least in terms of the private logic of the character. Students sometimes say to me, after coming up with a very improbable scene, 'But that really happened to me.' It doesn't matter. A narrative doesn't rely on truth, but believability. If you

wrote the COVID-19 plot in 1975, people would have said it was completely unbelievable. The fact that it has actually happened since makes no difference.

- Distinguish your character as particular – then *maintain* that particularity throughout the novel. Or at least until they undergo a thought-out change, if they are three-dimensional. I read many manuscripts in which the character starts off distinct, but ends up generic. All too often, they are generic in the first place.
- Character may be described by the author or narrator, but it is *also* what the character does, including what decisions they make, what they don't do, what they say, what they don't say, how they react.
- Character lies in *interactions* – it's hard to reveal character when the character is on their own without including long internal monologues – which was the main problem with my 'Charlie and the Hole' story.

## CONCLUSION:
## *The meaning of character*

I hope it is entirely clear now why plot and character cannot be separated. Change one and you change the other. A plot tells how a character responds psychologically to certain circumstances. They are a single organism.

Plot is what happens. Character is plot *inside the head.* The internal plot is at least as important as the external plot.

But they are both, in a sense, structured, with a beginning, middle and end.

If you have no internal plot in your book, you have a hollow book. If you have no external plot, you almost certainly have an unreadable book.

Both internal and external plot must be properly incorporated in a fully fledged story.

# 8

# *Change, Character and Plot in Real Life*

## HOW A NON-FICTION STORYCAN TRANSLATE INTO PLOT: *A personal journey, fictionalised*

'The plot twist of Boris Johnson getting the virus has come a bit earlier than I would have placed it, personally,' said the novelist Jonathan Coe in March 2020.

In his book *The Writer's Journey*, Christopher Vogler makes the suggestion that the 'hero's journey' – the mythic story structure – is not simply a construction that works for storytelling. It is, he says, 'an accurate map of the territory one must travel to become a writer or, for that matter, a human being'. He continues:

> The Hero's Journey and the Writer's Journey are one and the same. Anyone setting out to write a story soon

> encounters all the tests, trials, ordeals, joys, and rewards of the Hero's Journey... Writing is an often perilous journey inward to probe the depths of one's soul and bring back the Elixir of experience... Deadlines, editorial decisions, or the struggle to sell our work may be the Tests and Ordeals from which we seem to die but are Resurrected to write again. ['The Writer's Journey']

Vogler, I think, has struck on something important here. Stories are not just arrangements of fictional events, but mirrors of real life and the way we experience it – just as the three-act structure is a mirror of the human mind's patterning of thesis/antithesis/synthesis.

I once went on a men's retreat run by the cross-platform website Rebel Wisdom, which was patterned strictly on Joseph Campbell's hero's journey. During a weekend's experiential programme, I was led from *crossing the threshold* to the *ordeal* (in this case trauma), and then to *resurrection* and *return with the elixir* (the healing power of self-knowledge). This connection between an active therapeutic process and the act of storytelling suggests the existence of a deep pattern that, at the men's retreat, was being utilised for psychological and spiritual growth. Fiction, you might say, is a deep pattern of words, images and metaphors, which is another way of learning the same thing.

This mysterious relationship of fiction with real life is why good stories compel us so much.

And if it is true of everyone, it is certainly true of writers.

Speaking for myself, having suffered repeated bouts of acute mental illness, endured the suicide of my mother and been through two agonising divorces, I cannot help but be struck by Christopher Vogler's final paragraphs in *The Writer's Journey*.

He writes:

> Shamans have been called 'the wounded healers'... [They], like many writers, are prepared for their work by enduring terrible ordeals... They are taken apart and put back together again in a new way. In a sense they have died and been reborn, and this experience gives them special powers. Many writers come to their craft only after they have been shattered in this way...
>
> [Writers] ask the same ageless, childlike questions present by the myths: Who am I? Where did I come from? What happens when I die? What does it mean? Where do I fit in? Where am I bound on my own Hero's Journey? ['The Writer's Journey']

ooooo

Does story structure translate into real life?

As we've already observed, in our heads it does. We impose beginnings, middles and ends onto our life stories.

*In the beginning, I met your mother* (inciting incident). *At first we got on well* (dream stage), *then not so well* (frustration stage), *then we could barely talk to one another* (nightmare stage). *A* turning point *happened when I had an affair* (worst point). *After a final attempt at reconciliation* (final battle), *we separated, then divorced* (resolution).

As Scarlett Thomas points out in *Monkeys with Typewriters* (2012), life may be random, but we don't easily tolerate it that way.

When things go well for a long time, we are inclined to expect something bad to happen relatively soon.

A reversal, in other words.

We all have crises, and climaxes, and final battles – in our heads.

Life is also like story in that we often grow restless and bored when it isn't moving forward.

When *change* isn't happening, in other words.

We may wish to avoid all the pain that appears in stories, but we also want to become wise – and yet the pain is a necessary part of becoming wise.

Fictional stories act as a sort of painless substitute, a 'flight simulator' for life itself.

ooooo

I feel I have 'lived' story structure over and again – and continue to live it.

For instance, when I have ducked an important but crucial decision, I have sometimes fallen into mental chaos and depression.

In my head that is because I have failed a key stage of the hero's journey.

My life energies ossify when I feel I am living an inauthentic life.

All good stories with three-dimensional characters are about how to become complete and authentic.

Story structure, therefore, is my life's structure and my mind's structure, and my desire is the same as any fictional character's – to be, at the end of the story, a fully realised human being.

ooooo

Let's apply some of these ideas about fictional structure to a simple, first-person, *real-life* story.

Let's do it first in a three-act drama with a two-dimensional character.

That character being me.

The incident being real.

(Although I can be by no means sure that this event, which took place when I was in my mid-thirties, happened as I remember it – because memory always contains elements of fiction.)

Being a real-life situation, it does not contain the proper plot elements, except in a very rough form. In other words it is simply a 'story'.

But by (eventually) fictionalising it, I am going to 'tidy it up' into a proper plot, with a proper structure, by both adding and subtracting.

This is to demonstrate the point made by Nigel Watts in *Write a Novel: And Get It Published*: 'Although life rarely has a coherent plot, it often has the *makings of one* [my italics].'

For the purposes of this exercise, I am going to stop using the words 'plot' and 'story' interchangeably, and instead use them in their technical senses.

Just to recap, a *story* is a series of unstructured events bounded by a time sequence with no particular meaning. Just like real life.

A *plot* is a designed, structured series of occurrences that contains a conscious or unconscious meaning on the part of the author.

ooooo

This is the raw *story* as I remember it:

Scene: the late 1990s. I am walking into my house just off the then-seedy north end of the Portobello Road on a busy Saturday market day with my food shopping.

My house is empty. My wife and two children are out somewhere. Because my hands are filled with shopping bags, I briefly leave the door open behind me.

I put the bags down in the kitchen. When I return to close the door, I see that I have been followed into the house by a man, roughly in his thirties, who happens in this instance to be black. (This detail is relevant, as you will see.)

I challenge, automatically, angrily, the man who has followed me into my house.

Instead of retreating, he shocks me by calling me a racist and taking a threatening step towards me.

Suddenly, having been called a racist, I am on the defensive – but I am still angry.

I insist that I am not a racist, I am simply questioning his right to be in my house. I ask him, why he is there?

It registers now that he is big, and clearly much stronger than me.

I become nervous.

As I speak, the tone of my voice falters.

I'm no longer (in my mind) the brave, defiant householder facing down a cowardly intruder, who will retreat when faced with firm resolve.

I become positively frightened when the man grabs me round the neck, pinning my throat with the crook of his arm.

He is powerful. I am helpless.

In desperation, I make a strangled shout to my wife to call the police.

However, I know perfectly well she is not in the house, and he seems to guess that I am faking it.

He tightens his grip round my neck, choking me slightly, and I shut up.

Now with my bravado entirely spent, I plead with him not to hurt me and tell him to take whatever he likes from the house.

I am no longer the outraged householder, but a cowering, cornered animal.

And one suffering irrational pangs of guilt.

Because – perhaps absurdly – I am still not sure whether he is attacking me because he is a burglar or because he thinks I am a racist.

He tells me to give him all my money.

So that conundrum is pretty much solved.

(Unless he's burgling me *because I'm a racist* – I actually think for a moment.)

He briefly relaxes his grip so I can reach for my wallet.

I take it out of my pocket and offer it to him.

He tells me to take the money out of the wallet and hand that to him.

(A professional criminal's strategy. No wallet, no proof of theft.)

(At this point I no longer hold on to the supposition – unlikely in the first place – that he is attacking me and stealing from me because my challenge to him was rooted in racism.)

I give him the money.

He demands to know if there is any more money in the house.

I tell him, truthfully, that there isn't.

Then he pins me round the neck with his arm again, more tightly than ever.

He clearly doesn't believe me about there being no more money in the house.

He tells me, to my horror, that he is going to 'call some friends' to come to the house and assist him, and starts to make a call on his mobile phone.

Now panicking, I struggle to get away from him.

I am in fear of further violence or even my life.

To my surprise, since he is so much stronger than me, I manage to slip out of his grip.

I run desperately from the portico of the front door, through the hallway, corridor and into the kitchen.

In the door leading to the backyard from the kitchen, there is a key in the lock.

I pull the key out of the door, the plan being that I can lock my assailant in and be, at least temporarily, safe in the backyard, where I will call for help.

But when I get into the yard and turn to lock the door behind me, I realise/remember that there is *no keyhole on the outside*.

Only the inside.

In my panic, I had forgotten this crucial fact.

I stand there helplessly, feeling foolish now as well as afraid, and await my doom.

But the man does not come.

Gingerly returning into the house after some minutes have passed, I ascertain that he has left.

I realise now, in shock, that I have been so frightened that I have actually wet myself.

Humiliated, shaking and depressed, I clean myself up and call the police.

And what I keep thinking isn't: 'That was a lucky escape from a violent criminal,' but: 'Was I being racist when I challenged him?'

ooooo

So – let's take this real-life situation, and start to analyse it in terms of structure, character and theme, and see if we can turn it into a *fictional* drama *based on fact*.

You could say it is a satisfying drama already, and to a certain extent it is, because it is eventful and true and therefore of added interest.

But it is not a properly structured, satisfying drama.

It is a not a plot but a story – the story of the time I was attacked in my house.

It contains whatever meaning you project onto it, but it has no author who intended to communicate a particular meaning – even if that meaning is meaninglessness.

There are a number of ways of dividing the events up, so let's just envision it now as a three-act real-life drama.

Despite being a random, real-life event, it nevertheless contains the bare bones of a plot: a *protagonist*, an *antagonist*, cause and effect and a three-act structure, including an *inciting incident*, a *crisis/worst point* and a *climax*.

## ACT ONE

The ordinary world/stasis – I come in from shopping.

This is disrupted by the inciting incident, the arrival of the intruder.

### ACT TWO

The long second act – perils and adventures, back and forth. He threatens me. I beg him not to hurt me. He asks me to hand over my wallet. I try to give it to him, but then he tells me to keep the wallet and just give him the money. He still has me by the throat. I give him the money, begging him not to hurt me. He now says he's going to call 'some friends'. This act concludes here, with the worst point, the crisis, when I think I am going to be hurt, or even killed.

### ACT THREE

The climax. I struggle to escape – and to my surprise, I do. I run to the backyard, in my mind at least pursued by my antagonist, where I await my fate. However, the antagonist does not appear.

I realise, humiliated and afraid, that I have urinated from pure fear.

A reversal has occurred – from militant householder protecting his home to terrified victim, shamed by his own bladder.

End of story.

ooooo

Now, leaving the three-act structure intact, let's analyse it, psychologically, from the point of view of the protagonist – me.

Let's take me to be a purely two-dimensional character – that is, one who does not change or show internal contradictions.

I think – or thought, at that time – of myself as a reasonably brave person, and certainly a passionate one.

I at least *value* courage highly.

After the intrusion, at the conclusion of the first act, I react, in my mind, as a reasonably brave person might have done, at least if I want to flatter myself. (Others might see it as foolishness or rashness – or even, as my antagonist suggests, racism.)

That is, I forcefully challenge the antagonist.

The point is, all the reader of the story has to judge my character on are my *actions*, which are confrontational.

That is, instead of realising at once that I am faced with someone of superior strength and probably malign intent (and therefore adopting a passive or reasonable response to save myself as best I can), I become emotional and aggressive.

However you judge my action, my aggression says something about this character – me – because other people might well have reacted in a different way.

Perhaps more politely, perhaps more sensibly.

The arrival of the intruder is the *inciting incident* in the story and represents my first crisis, the problem, which propels me into the second act.

I have suddenly found myself in *the woods*, that is, unexplored territory.

I have acquired a strong *desire* – to escape the intruder unharmed.

That is my quest, my *overarching goal*, triggered by the inciting incident.

At this point there are a number of ways the story *could* go – in fiction.

But my first attempt to solve the problem of the interloper – by challenging him aggressively – has failed.

Now I am really stuck in the hole.

And I don't know how – or if – I am going to get out again.

In Act Two, which has now begun, since we have had the *inciting incident*/first *crisis*, we can see that the first of two *reversals* has taken place.

I have gone from being theatrically brave to being theatrically afraid.

Then the interloper, who has cast himself at first as the victim – 'You're a racist' – has revealed himself simply to be a robber, since he is using violence and demanding money.

He is not, after all, an aggrieved victim of my prejudice but a violent criminal.

This second act culminates in the *worst point*, when I think I am going to die at the hands of the man and his (possibly imaginary) helpers.

At this second moment of crisis (*the* crisis), I make a *choice* – remember, 'crisis' implies 'choice' – and decide to try to break away.

In Act Three, I am (at least in my imagination) heading for the *final battle* with my antagonist, after which the plot will resolve.

However, in dramatic terms, the story now peters into bathos, or even black comedy.

Instead of confronting 'the villain' for the final battle, I find I have added to my cowardice by absurdity – I don't realise that there isn't a keyhole outside.

And the final humiliation – I have pissed myself.

Perhaps this is actually a satisfactory plot. Some might say so. And it kind of works as a reflection of real life. It's more Raymond Carver than *Die Hard* – but there's nothing wrong with that.

But it is not a classic plot.

If I am a two-dimensional character, nothing follows from this sequence of actions.

I do not change my view of myself or of the world.

I have learned nothing (except that I am easily scared).

If something similar happened again, I would probably react in the same way.

I would be neither more nor less brave, cowardly or gullible.

I am not a hero, or anything like.

The antagonist, in the meanwhile, is barely any more dimensional than I am.

He has shown himself to be cunning, by claiming to be a victim of racism, but otherwise he is a stereotype, and a negative one, because he is a black male in Notting Hill, in a part of the area known for a high crime rate.

However, he also had choices to make.

He could have pursued me to the back of the house, and done – what?

Who knows?

But it was a possibility.

ooooo

This is a real-life story, but not really a plot, because although it is causally connected – one thing leads to another – it has no particular *meaning*.

Remember, in a classic plot the *climax* (the final act) represents the meaning or theme of the story.

So now, keeping as closely to the real-life story as possible, I'm going to try to develop the story into a proper plot. (You may continue to prefer the original, in all its open-endedness. Which is fair enough. But in a classic plot, more is required.)

Let's assume we have set our protagonist up, through backstory, in Act One, as a campaigner against racism, a left-wing radical.

He has marched on many occasions as a teenager for Rock Against Racism, and considers the police to be systemic oppressors of racial minorities.

His assumption is that reportedly high levels of street crime among the Afro-Caribbean community in the area are propaganda – a product of racism.

He sees himself as a good, tolerant, rational, non-violent and brave person, always on the side of the underdog.

The antagonist remains unchanged – although perhaps we can also envisage him as not merely the interloper, but as a representation of the protagonist's own suppressed violent impulses and his own latent racism. His Shadow, as the Jungians would have it.

After all, would the protagonist have reacted the same if the interloper had been a middle-aged white man wearing spectacles and a tweed jacket?

Some of the assumptions he has about himself are about to be challenged in this new version of the drama.

Our protagonist's *want* is immediately established by the arrival of the burglar.

(We can give our protagonist a name now. Let's call him 'Owen'.)

In real life, there is only one *want* (at least consciously) – to get out of the situation and return life to a balanced, stable, safe condition.

To escape, in other words.

In the fictional version, we can add on some other *wants*.

Perhaps the protagonist wants to show how 'tolerant' and 'understanding' he is.

He might be less hot-headed.

He might be less judgemental.

His immediate desire might be not so much to get out of the situation, but to prove that he is a good person, to show that he understands that the interloper has only been driven to this unfortunate action by systemic racism and poverty.

Perhaps he is not as intimidated as the real-life protagonist (me), and is calm and collected in the face of the threat.

And perhaps his *want* – to be tolerant and civilised – turns out to be very different from his *need* – which we will find out at the conclusion of the story.

Perhaps, in fact, he is someone who is the opposite of who he thinks he is.

Now we can start to build the drama.

Note the plot – as that is what this is becoming, as opposed to a story – is highly dependent on the character of the protagonist.

In Act Two, Owen starts desperately to catalogue all his anti-racist activities and political persuasions, hoping it will win sympathy with the intruder.

He says he is a pacifist, utterly opposed to violence.

Then he talks of his wife and child, trying now to engage the humanity of the antagonist.

Both strategies fail. But they reveal something about the character of the protagonist.

The intruder starts talking to a 'friend' on the phone, summoning him to the address.

Owen starts to panic.

Then he finally breaks away and runs to the backyard.

He starts to yell for someone to call the police, hoping a neighbour will hear.

Unlike in real life, however, in this fictional plot the intruder follows him.

They face one another, enclosed in a tiny space.

Unbeknown to the intruder, however, Owen has found a weapon – a heavy poker that happened to be lying in the backyard.

Before the intruder has had a chance to do or say anything, Owen, on impulse and in desperation, smashes the intruder across the head with the poker.

The intruder collapses to the floor, bleeding and unconscious.

Then, instead of running back into the house, locking the door behind him, in order to call the police, Owen strikes the man again in fury.

And again and again, until the intruder is no threat, bleeding and unconscious.

But still Owen continues in a frenzy.

Until he has killed the intruder.

Owen stands and contemplates the bloody mess at his feet.

And, to his surprise, instead of feeling guilt or regret, he feels more alive than he has ever felt before.

The avowed anti-racist and pacifist has become a killer, someone in touch with his dark side.

And what's more, he's enjoyed becoming a killer.

Instead of soiling himself, he finds that he has a slight erection.

And this narrative is now a plot rather than story – because it reveals some new layer of meaning, as opposed to being simply a series of causally linked events.

ooooo

One could go further still, and develop the character of the antagonist a little further.

Let's call him Kingsley – street name Kingzy.

He's had a bad day.

His mother is ill, his rent is overdue and he's under a lot of stress one way or the other. And he's just lost £100 in a card game, during which he was sure his fellow players were cheating.

Perhaps Kingzy is following Owen into the house because Owen has dropped something – a gift for his daughter, a miniature Beanie Baby toy (they were all the rage in the 1990s).

Kingzy's intention is simply to return the Beanie Baby, then be on his way.

Kingzy is more or less law-abiding, although he has a difficult family background and smokes more weed than is probably good for him. At the moment he has drunk a fairly large amount of beer, which, since he is on medication for depression, makes him somewhat unstable.

He is certainly not a habitual criminal.

He walks into the house, and is about to give Owen back the tiny toy, when, challenged, he realises that Owen has automatically and outrageously assumed he is a robber.

Owen's defensive aggression (he gets angry in this version of the plot, as I did in real life) raises Kingzy's hackles – drunk and edgy as he is.

Our 'antagonist' has had to put up with this kind of racist stereotyping all his life – and finally, at this moment, he's suddenly sick to death of it.

It's been a bad day, and everyone has a breaking point.

If people are going to think he's a robber, even when he's trying to be helpful, then what the hell?

He might as well *be* a robber.

Now – furious, and terrified that Owen might call the police on him, even though he is innocent (so far) – Kingzy, in a panic, grabs Owen round the neck.

He doesn't know what to do next, but he finds himself caught inside a story. That is to say, he would feel ridiculous if he simply let go, said 'sorry', and left the house quietly.

On impulse, he asks for money. Why not? Owen thought he was a robber even when he hadn't done anything wrong, in fact was trying to help. And he is £100 out of pocket after his unfairly fixed game of cards.

Now he might be able to pay his rent.

Might as well be hanged for a sheep as for a lamb.

So Kingzy takes the money. Fifty quid. Not worth the effort.

But then, once again, he doesn't know what to do next.

Because to let go and simply walk away is to reveal – to himself as much as anyone else – that he is, or has become on the instant, a violent robber.

Also, he needs more cash to meet his rent bill. (He tells himself he'll pay Owen back next time he has better luck at cards.)

Uncertain what to do, and playing for time, Kingzy demands more money and makes a fake phone call.

When Owen wriggles to get out of his grip, Kingzy sees a

way out of his dilemma and lets – accidentally on purpose – Owen run away.

Seeing Owen's obvious terror he stares in horror at the stolen £50 in his hand. In the corridor he notices a pair of baby's bootees lying on the floor.

He is suddenly struck by remorse and shame.

He decides to follow Owen, give him back his money and the Beanie Baby, apologise for his rash behaviour, then make a hasty exit.

Apart from anything else Kingzy doesn't want to reinforce any negative racist stereotypes.

He edges anxiously into the backyard, hoping to reassure Owen that he meant no harm and return his money.

But before he has a chance to explain, Owen springs from behind a makeshift shed and beats him to death.

Then, as Owen stands over Kingzy's prostrate body, breathing heavily, he sees something in the intruder's open, bloody palm.

The Beanie Baby that Owen dropped earlier.

ooooo

In the example above we can see how real life can be built on to construct a plot and how character mutates plot.

With the exception of Karl Ove Knausgaard and a few others, real life alone does not provide enough material for a complete work of fiction – but life definitely provides promising material for scenes within a narrative.

# 9

## *Conclusion: The Rebirth of the Author*

In conclusion, I will reiterate what I stated at the start of this book.

Storytelling is a mystery – but it's not a *total* mystery.

What I hope I have given you in this book is not a toolkit for constructing a pre-planned object, but a list of ingredients for preparing a dish. How you combine them and how you cook them are up to you. A light, sweet soufflé or a salad of bitter herbs.

I have tried to keep the subject matter as simple as possible, but I still find myself half inclined to reduce the whole topic to Peggy Ramsay's 'two or three little surprises followed every now and then by a bigger surprise'.

Which is only to restate that there has been a deadly overcomplication of the craft of storytelling in the service of an industry that feeds greedily on that overcomplication.

And I am reluctant to add to that process in any way.

Perhaps even this short book you find to be overly confusing, or even long-winded. I have no problem with that.

I don't expect you to 'get' every word of it or even to be interested in every word of it.

I find myself in agreement with Malcolm Bradbury, who, shortly after he set up his famous course in creative writing at the University of East Anglia in 1970, remarked to his students: 'Ninety per cent of what you hear in this room will be useless, but the ten per cent will be invaluable. And it will be a different ten per cent for every person.'

ooooo

Above all, the spirit behind this book pleads in favour of a shift in responsibility for writing a novel from the teacher to the student. From the creative-writing industry to the lonely passion of the writer.

Roland Barthes talked of the 'death of the author'. I am agitating for the *rebirth* of the author – away from classes, courses and academic over-schooling.

It is YOU who must write this novel. It is YOU who must come up with the energy and imagination and fire for it. It is YOU who must have the wisdom and determination to keep going.

Creative-writing teachers can't give you any of that.

They can only give you hints, which you are always at liberty to ignore.

That's what this book is – a book of clues, not rules or principles.

Do not let these hints and clues dominate your writing.

Only allow them to *inform* it.

The problems you face are the problems every writer has faced since the beginning of written human history.

Doubt. Fear of the blank page. Confusion. Insecurity. Blockage. Solitude.

These are not problems to which solutions can be conveniently offered.

They are realities that every writer must grapple with.

Struggling with them does not mean you have no talent as a writer.

It *may* do.

But then again, it may not.

ooooo

Yes – it is useful, for the reader's sake, to have a clear beginning, middle and end.

But you, as a writer, are free.

Without that freedom, you are not a writer or an artist, but someone who paints by numbers.

Such a technique may produce a pretty picture – but the writer's job is the creation of meaning, not the making of a pretty picture.

You are, and must be, a wild creature – not a tame animal.

But exactly because art is wild and untrammelled, it has to be tempered by structure and craft.

So go into the woods or into the void, or whatever you

want to call it, with realistic expectations, but also with an understanding of your craft as well as hope and idealism.

What you are doing – or trying to do – is not simply a hobby (although it may be that too).

It is *important.*

Perhaps one of the most important things a human being can ever do for themselves and for the community at large.

For *storytelling* – not prostitution – is the oldest profession.

So – take yourself and your writing seriously.

Respect your vision.

Face down the chaos.

Get to the end – somehow.

You may fail.

The odds are certainly against you.

But – so what?

The odds have been against pretty much every writer who ever lived.

And they did it anyway.

Because they were writers.

As Randle McMurphy, in Ken Kesey's great novel *One Flew Over the Cuckoo's Nest* (1962), yells, sweating and exhausted, after hopelessly trying to remove the impossibly heavy control panel from the hydrotherapy room of the asylum in which he is being confined:

'But I tried, though. Goddammit, I sure as hell did that much, now, didn't I?'

THE END

# APPENDIX I

## *Structure Grid*

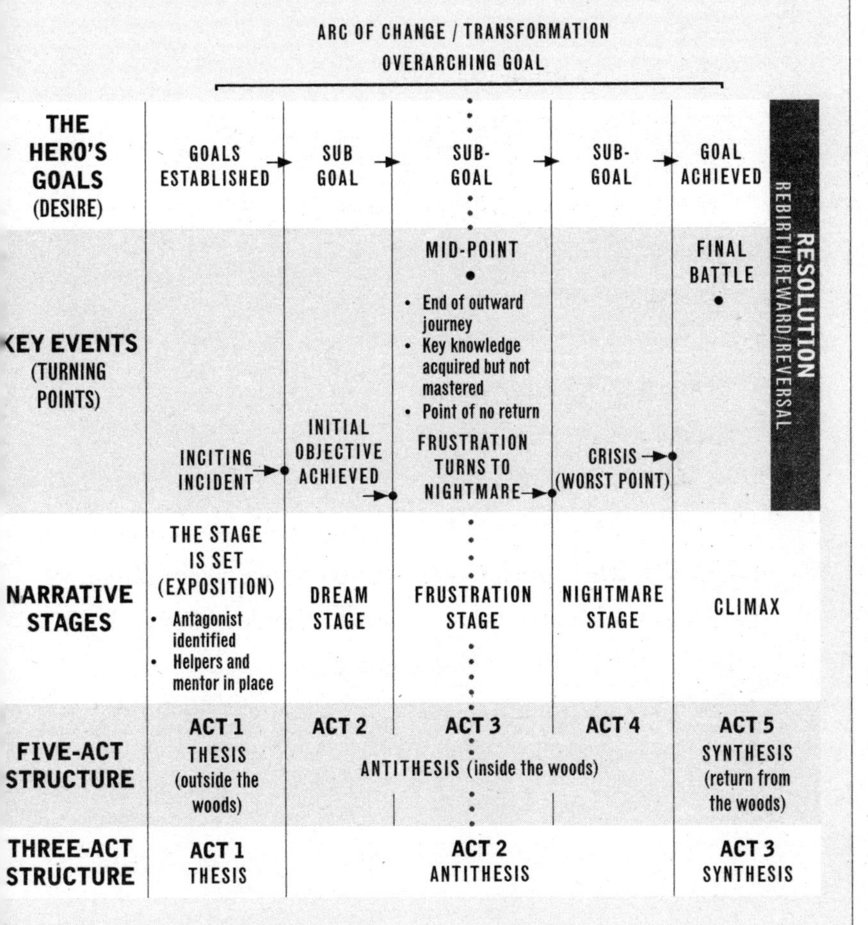


FIGURE 9: The author's attempt to define story structure

# APPENDIX 2

## *The Mid-Point*

The *mid-point* is most visible in Shakespearean dramas and mainstream Hollywood films.

In the case of *Macbeth*, it's simply that there is no going back. Macbeth actually states the fact baldly:

> I am in blood
> Stepped in so far that should I wade no more,
> Returning were as tedious as go o'er. [III, iv, 136–8]

In *Hamlet*, the mid-point comes when the players perform *The Murder of Gonzago* in front of the king and the court, and Claudius's guilt is confirmed for Hamlet beyond any doubt. After this, the time for procrastination is over. Hamlet's mind is made up.

At *King Lear*'s mid-point, on the heath, Lear finally recognises his fatal character flaw – spiritual pride (the *mirror moment*). He begins to discover humility as he reaches out to the wretched Poor Tom:

Oh I have ta'en
Too little care of this! [III, iv, 32–3]

Here are a some famous cinematic mid-points:

Rick in *Casablanca* (1942) experiences his *mirror moment* after Ilsa walks out on him in disgust, leaving him asking the perennial dramatic question: 'Who am I?'

After llsa tells him that he's not the Rick she used to know, Rick is cast into despair, and sees for the first time what he has become – cynical and bitter.

He then begins to experiment with acting for the common good rather than being out for himself.

He is starting to transform – to move away from the Rick who uttered the words, earlier in the film, 'I stick my neck out for no man.'

In *Joker* (2019) Arthur Fleck sees himself humiliated on TV by his erstwhile hero, host Murray Franklin. This is the moment, as it were, that his soul finally and irremediably curdles.

It's the moment in *Jaws* (1975) when 'we're going to need a bigger boat'.

When the *Titanic* hits the iceberg.

When, in *Alien* (1979), the creature bursts out of Kane's stomach.

When, halfway through *The Queen* (2006), Queen Elizabeth discovers empathy after a stag she saw in a forest is hunted down and killed.

When, halfway through *Parasite* (2019), the family find the hider in the basement – and the host family return.

When, halfway through every Pixar film, the central characters start to collaborate.

Although it is often less easily identifiable, the mid-point can also be located in novels.

The mid-point for Pip in *Great Expectations* comes as he shamefully turns his back on his beloved stepfather Joe Gargery when he visits him in London, and, two chapters later, when he meets Estella as a grown woman for the first time.

It's important to note that a mid-point in a novel can occupy several chapters, and more than one event, and is not always exactly in the middle, since there is such a lot of room for novelists to fill space with voice and description.

When Pip sees Estella again, she still treats Pip with disdain – he has not grown up. He is still, in his own words, a 'wretched boy' – but now he knows it (mirror moment). Accordingly, Estella doesn't accept him until the end of the book, when his transformation from boy to man, from ego-driven self to a fully integrated person, is complete.

In *Pride and Prejudice*, the mid-point is the chapter in which Darcy first proposes to Elizabeth and she rejects him, citing his pride and arrogance, his interference in her sister's romance with Bingley and his cruelty to Wickham. That refusal propels him into writing the letter in which he reveals the truth about Wickham but admits to meddling in Bingley's business. That, in turn, leads Elizabeth to realise she's been prejudiced towards Darcy, which had blinded her to the truth about Wickham.

There are countless other examples. Halfway through *Us* (2014) by David Nicholls, the protagonist, Douglas, sets off to find his son, and thus, hopefully, win back his wife.

In *The Great Gatsby* (1925) we witness Gatsby's crisis as we intuit that he will be unable to make his dream a reality with regard to Daisy. For the first time, he takes her into his vast, palatial home and tries to demonstrate to her his wealth and success. The reader knows, as Daisy helplessly pretends to admire his expensive shirts, and mysteriously bursts into tears, that the love affair is unlikely to end well.

Modernist writers who eschew such structural conceits still have a habit of writing them into their stories. Eimear McBride's unapologetically modernist *A Girl Is a Half-Formed Thing* (2013), which is otherwise more or less structureless – intentionally, one imagines – has an almost exact mid-point crisis when girl, who was raped by her uncle earlier in the book, meets him again, and they have an ambiguous sexual dalliance in his car.

# APPENDIX 3

## *The Shape of Stories – Ten Novels*

In this section, I have tried to X-ray a number of well-known novels in order to reveal their underlying structure and character design.

I have used a mix of both classical and mythic theory to describe the structures.

These two systems overlap and intermix, but they do also have separate parts.

I have used **bold** for classical-theory terms (three and five-act structure) and *italic* for mythic-theory terms. Some terms are stated or implied in both systems, and I have left those unchanged.

No comprehensive blueprint for a story can ever be possible, but, in incorporating mythic and classical structure, we cover as many bases as we can without – hopefully – over-complicating things.

Fractal theory has been left out of the equation, not

because it isn't a profound analysis but because it works far better for screenplays and drama than for fiction. And because it would make this section (with the addition of a *third* template) impossibly convoluted.

## *Great Expectations*

### CHARLES DICKENS (1861; 412 PP.)

*Great Expectations* is in many ways the model of a classic story, although it is long (183,000 words) and contains a large cast of characters and a number of substantial subplots.

It starts with Pip – shy, passive – as a young boy having a terrifying encounter with an escaped criminal on the marshes near his adoptive father's blacksmith's forge. We might mistake this dramatic moment as an **inciting incident**, but it is not. It is simply sets up what is to come in the last part of the story. It does not set the action in train. I give events like this the name 'plot bomb' – an event designed to explode much later in the story.

At the book's heart it is a simple *quest* story. Pip acquires a profound desire – to win the girl, Estella, whom he falls in love with at the eccentric Miss Havisham's when he is still just a boy. In order to achieve this goal, he knows he has to become a gentleman, since, when they meet at Miss Havisham's, Estella scorns him for his common background and lack of sophistication: 'He calls the knaves jacks, this boy!'

*This* is the **inciting incident**, and incites the desire, or want, that drives the bulk of the action for the **protagonist** throughout the novel.

The *call to adventure* comes when he is informed that he has a secret benefactor (whom he assumes is Miss Havisham) who has given him a large sum of money in order that he might become a gentleman. He thus accepts the opportunity to travel to London to seek his fortune, and win Estella, leaving behind the simple country life he was born to, and the people who love him most: his aunt's husband, Joe Gargery, and the schoolteacher, Biddy. This is a critical choice, a key turning point.

With the leaving of London, the *threshold has been crossed* – the threshold between the *ordinary world* and the *special world*. Pip enters the *void*, a crucible in which he will be remade.

The **second act** commences when Pip arrives in London and starts to try to acquire the qualities of a gentleman. In character terms, his confidence begins to grow, but so do his contradictions. Who is he? A simple country boy or an elegant gentleman?

At this point he acquires *allies* (Herbert Pocket, John Wemmick, Mr Wopsle) and a dark *mentor* of sorts in the lugubrious lawyer Mr Jaggers. In Act Three of a five-act paradigm, things are going well. His training is successful, he acquires an elegant wardrobe and good friends. We are in the **dream stage**. He is coming closer to his overarching goal, or superobjective – Estella.

His pursuit of Estella continues. Then comes the **mid-point** of the story (or the *ordeal*), which actually straddles several chapters. Firstly, when Joe Gargery comes to visit him in London, Pip essentially rejects him, ashamed of his step-parent's coarse behaviour. This is his **mirror moment**: 'What have I become?' Then he returns to Miss Havisham's, where he is led to believe by Miss Havisham that Estella is his destiny, and where he meets Estella again for the first time as a full-grown woman, and finds that he is more desperately in love than ever (**point of no return**). But she is cool and dismissive towards him. The **frustration stage** is well under way. From here on in, things must get worse before they get better.

Bentley Drummle, Pip's antagonist and *enemy*, a rich, unpleasant snob, is now firmly established in the narrative. Pip finds out that he is also courting Estella. The **worst point/crisis** comes, like the **mid-point**, in two instalments. First, with the arrival of Magwitch, a common criminal on the run from the police, who represents everything Pip had been trying to escape. Devastatingly for Pip, it is Magwitch, not Miss Havisham, who turns out to be his benefactor. We are at the first part of the **crisis**, which seems to signal the death of all hope. But Pip's character is undergoing a change. At first horrified by the convict, and helping him only out of guilt and the desire to get rid of him, he begins to feel compassion and even love for Magwitch – who is not only Pip's opposite, but Estella's. Here is the collision of opposites working its magic. This is a key part of his transformation into a fully integrated character.

The second part of the **worst point** comes a few chapters later, when Pip discovers that Estella is to wed Bentley Drummle (who, it later turns out, she is only marrying as a means of punishing Pip, as she has been taught by the bitter Miss Havisham to punish all men).

It is here, at this elongated **worst point**, that Pip finally turns his heart around. Instead of being ruled by his egotistic desire, he discovers the humility and the generosity to thank Magwitch and help him escape. He is now capable of seeing the goodness in the rough-and-ready convict. Helped by Herbert Pocket, his chief *ally*, and in a state of maximum jeopardy, they try to make a run for it by rowing out to meet a packet steamer leaving London and placing Magwitch on it so he can escape. Compeyson, who is Magwitch's *enemy/* antagonist, pursues them with the police. We are deep into the **climax** of the story. At the climactic moment, the boat capsizes and Compeyson and Magwitch struggle in a deadly embrace.

Past the climactic moment we reach **resolution**. The story is nearly completed when Pip tenderly looks after the ailing Magwitch before his death. Then he returns to Kent (fulfilling the three-act country–city–country paradigm). He has become complete and is sadder and wiser, but surrounded by those who love him – Biddy and Joe, who are now married. He is, in other words, reborn.

But what of his original desire? What of Estella, the wellspring of all the action in the first place?

In what is something of a tacked-on, but nonetheless satisfying ending (in the original, Estella and Pip were not reconciled), Pip meets Estella at Satis House, where they first met, and they come together, never to be parted, both of them changed and chastened, brought down from their pride and redeemed from their flaws.

Thus there is a happy ending of sorts. Pip's reward comes for all the trials he has suffered. He has all the hallmarks of a fully fledged character, on a journey of change – from innocence to experience, from pride to humility, from conscious want to unconscious need, from home into the woods and back home again. His antagonist, Estella, has also changed by the end of the book – like Pip, older, sadder and wiser. And, we hope, more complete.

## *The Great Gatsby*

F. SCOTT FITZGERALD (1925; 115 PP.)

*Gatsby* is a slightly atypical novel in that the first-person narrator, Nick Carraway, is not the **protagonist**, who is Gatsby himself. Nick tells us to trust him because 'I am one of the few honest people that I have ever known.' It is a book, in a way, *about* storytelling, most particularly the story Gatsby creates for himself, and how America itself is becoming obsessed by false surfaces, including surface personalities with made-up stories as a 'front' for darker or more banal realities. It is, as much as anything else, about a *world*, the world of New York's pleasure-seeking socialites of the 1920s.

Much of the first part of the book is not about Gatsby at all, but about Carraway, the world of West Egg and the more fashionable East Egg (retreats for the wealthy in easy reach of Manhattan). You might locate the **inciting incident** in the moment when Nick sights Daisy Buchanan in her husband Tom Buchanan's house, in a famous, ethereal scene in which the wind swirls around her and Nick's love interest, Jordan Baker – depicting them as half-real angels.

This is where the story really starts – because the story is the story of Daisy and Gatsby. The plot is driven entirely by Gatsby's desire – for Daisy. In that sense, you could also say that the **inciting incident** happens long before the book begins – when Daisy and Gatsby part, years previously, leaving the impoverished Gatsby desperate to make something of himself and win Daisy back (very much echoes of *Great Expectations* here).

Other than Gatsby's desire for Daisy, there isn't much that is real about him as a character. His past is murky, to say the least, and shot through with lies and corruption. He covers up any character traits with a mask of charm and affability and sociability. His conversation is peppered with clichés and catchphrases. He is, in essence, a two-dimensional character. He is asked to change by the events of the narrative ('Abandon your foolish desire for this worthless woman!' the reader may prompt, desperately), but he cannot or will not. But we care about him all the same – because of the tragic purity of his desire. And because we care, we also pity him as he stays hopelessly true to Daisy right up to his fatal end.

It isn't until Chapter 3 that Carraway goes to one of Gatsby's parties, and we hear rumours about him – stories, in other words. That he killed someone once, that he was educated at Oxford, that he is involved with organised crime. Gatsby hints at the heart of the plot when he tells Nick about 'something very sad that had happened to me long ago'.

At a lunch with Gatsby and a disreputable character called Meyer Wolfsheim, Nick learns that Gatsby met Daisy five years earlier, and that the only reason Gatsby bought his enormous mansion was so that he could be close to Daisy.

Gatsby arranges to meet Daisy at Nick's house. Gatsby, at first terrified, becomes elated. Awestruck, he dazedly shows Daisy around his vast mansion. Almost precisely halfway through the book, at the **mid-point**, Daisy is shown into Gatsby's bedroom, where he tries to impress her, somewhat pathetically, by showing her his collection of expensive shirts. Daisy, unaccountably, begins to cry.

At this point it is clear that the relationship is not going to turn out well. And Carraway comments: 'I could have sworn I heard the owl-eyed man break into ghostly laughter.' It is the **point of no return** for Gatsby. It is also the moment which marks his becoming truly proactive, rather than passive. Now he has found Daisy, he has to win her.

The **crisis** for Gatsby comes when his antagonist, Tom Buchanan, humiliates him and demonstrates his absolute confidence that Daisy will stay with him, despite Gatsby's protestations to the contrary. Tom is so sure of it that he insists that Daisy drive off with Gatsby. At this point, Gatsby is defeated, whether or not he knows it – because Buchanan is right: Daisy will never leave him.

The **climax**, this being a tragedy, does not come with the final triumphant reunion of Gatsby and Daisy and the destruction of the awful Tom. Instead Daisy runs over Tom Buchanan's mistress in Gatsby's car, and Tom fires up his mistress's husband, Wilson, claiming that it was Gatsby who killed his wife. Wilson then shoots Gatsby in revenge, believing him to be the driver. Gatsby remains true to Daisy, never revealing that it was in fact she who was driving the car, an act of loyalty that costs him his life. After his death, Tom and Daisy return to their life of privilege somewhere offstage. Gatsby's story will end up as just a little anecdote for them, to be told at glamorous dinner parties.

Nobody comes to Gatsby's funeral. No one hears from Daisy and Tom again. This is the tragic **resolution**.

This, of course, is mere plot – necessary but not sufficient. The greatness of the novel lies in the profundity of its writing and all the multiple meanings it might contain, being endlessly open to interpretation. But a plot it needs all the same, as well as compelling characters – and Fitzgerald has constructed both beautifully.

## *Bridget Jones's Diary*
### HELEN FIELDING (1996; 310 PP.)

There is no doubt about who the **protagonist** is – as in most first-person narratives. Bridget Jones is a thirty-something woman trying to be both professionally and romantically successful. Bridget's comic, doofy, vulnerable 'voice' carries the book, but all the staging posts of a plot are in place – sort of. We immediately care about her because, in the space of her diary, she can be honest, funny – and flawed. From the get-go, we see beneath the mask she has to present at work – and to her parents, and to her potential lovers – very clearly and simply.

Her desires at the beginning of the story are straightforward: they are directly stated at length in a list titled 'I Will'. To lose weight. To give up smoking. To drink less. To 'form functional relationship with responsible adult'. To have a successful career.

We meet her on New Year's Day as she endures one of her stuffy parents' parties. Here she meets Mark Darcy, a friend from childhood, now grown up, whom she writes off as being as uninteresting as her parents and their tedious suburban friends.

Fielding puts into place Bridget's *allies* – her friends Sharon, Tom and Jude.

After this the central story gets under way as she starts to flirt with Daniel Cleaver, her charming, caddish boss at the publishing firm where she works. The **inciting incident** is clear – she sleeps with Daniel Cleaver 20 per cent of the way through the book. After this the **dream stage** unfolds – things go well, their affair develops and Bridget announces to her diary that she is in love. Her desire has been gloriously fulfilled.

But the novel – obviously – can't end there. At the **mid-point** (which comes thirty pages later than the precise arithmetical middle) she discovers Cleaver has a girlfriend whom he is going to marry. Bridget is devastated and has her **mirror moment** – she intuits that she is going to end up as a lonely spinster. Her diet and smoking regimes collapse. The **nightmare stage** is under way.

After this, the story deflates somewhat, structure-wise, and ends up having to rely more or less on Bridget's (very likeable) voice/character, and an unlikely subplot involving her mother, who leaves her father for a romantic chancer called Julio, and a series of failed dates as well as consolatory outings with her *allies*/friends. This, for me, was the least successful part of the novel – a very common problem for a writer trying to get through the **long second act**. Not that it stopped the book becoming a massive bestseller.

The **crisis** doesn't actually come until a few pages before the end of the book, when Bridget finds herself back with her parents, facing another Christmas alone. 'Oh God, I'm so lonely,' she writes in her diary.

But this is not a tragedy, and even with only a few pages to go, we know the book is not going to end there. There has been some intermittent back-and-forth between Bridget and Mark Darcy in the meantime, but not in a way that is entirely central to the narrative. The **climax** and **resolution** arrive right at the end of the book, only a few pages after the **crisis**, with Mark Darcy arriving in her parents' garden on Christmas Day, after Julio, drunk, has appeared with the intention of winning back 'his woman' from Bridget's father, who has returned home.

Mark announces that the police are there to arrest Julio. Mark announces that he is taking Bridget away to spend Christmas with him. She swooningly agrees. **Resolution** and theme – true love conquers all. Bridget gets what she announced she desired in the first few pages – to 'form functional relationship with responsible adult'. She initially got what she wanted – Daniel Cleaver (glamorous, charismatic, unreliable) – but she ended up with what she needed, Mark Darcy (decent, a bit dull, someone who truly loves her). And, in choosing the latter over the former, she has grown up. A bit, anyway.

It is a classic love story (based, of course, on the ur-classic of the genre, *Pride and Prejudice*), and its happy ending and charming voice guaranteed its huge success. But when it was bought by production company Working Title Films and adapted into a screenplay by Richard Curtis, Andrew Davies and Fielding herself, a number of understandable changes were made to improve the shortcomings of the book's structure.

In the film, Darcy essentially rejects Bridget as a potential love interest in the opening scene far more firmly than he does in the book (just as Mr Darcy rejects Lizzy Bennet in *Pride and Prejudice*).

Darcy, in this version, also has another love interest, Natasha, who is introduced in Act Two, thus creating jeopardy for Bridget. Darcy is much more present in the second half of the film than he is in the equivalent section of the novel, since he and Bridget represent the main story, whereas Fielding drops this thread somewhat in the book in favour of a subplot about her mother and a Portuguese tour operator. The **crisis, climax** and **resolution** are much less rushed than in the book, with final scenes including a dinner party with Bridget's *allies* to which Darcy turns up to help cook the meal. Cleaver then arrives and has a fight with Darcy. Darcy injures Cleaver. Then Darcy walks away in apparent disgust when Bridget goes to help Cleaver instead of him.

But Bridget then rejects Cleaver as well. She realises her mistake in spurning Darcy, then goes in search of him, but finds he is with Natasha. Darcy and Natasha are about to announce their engagement and move to New York together – the **crisis**.

Bridget's *allies* descend to console her with a surprise trip to Paris, but, just as they are about to leave, Darcy arrives, having realised where true love lies. We are at the **climax**. Bridget, thrilled, decides to go and change into some sexier clothes, but Mark finds an old entry in her diary in which she has written horrible things about him.

He leaves. She chases after him, in the snow, semi-clad. You could say that she is also now emotionally naked. She finally catches him. But it turns out that he wasn't trying to leave – he had gone to buy her a new diary. They kiss. **Resolution** and *reward*.

Both film and book were successful, but the film gives much more primacy to story structure. The plot is much more important in the movie, because, in a novel, character can be expressed far more directly in the form of thought – in this case transcribed into diary entries.

## *On Chesil Beach*

### IAN MCEWAN (2007; 166 PP.)

*On Chesil Beach* is essentially a classically constructed 'long' short story, or novella, interspersed with flashback portraits of the dual **protagonists** and the early-1960s English world they are trapped in. It's only 40,000 words long – half that of the average novel. Structurally and in terms of subject matter it is somewhat similar to David Nicholls's *Us* (see below) – though the tone is entirely different – since both start with a crisis moment in a marriage and then keep cutting back to show how the relationship developed in the first place.

The key question is established by page 6. What will happen when the newly-weds, Edward and Florence, on their honeymoon, have sex? For she is horrified by the idea and he cannot wait. The collision of opposites is plainly foreshadowed.

The surprise of the **inciting incident** – which occurs roughly thirty pages in – is that, after an uncomfortable dinner in their hotel room, she, not he, takes the initiative and leads him to the bed.

Then McEwan teases us – makes us wait for the outcome – by introducing a series of flashbacks about how the two of them met and their individual lives. It is suddenly no longer about the impending dilemma of the **protagonists**, but about their parents, about growing up and the world of 1960s bourgeois England. Thus it becomes at least as much about character as about plot. Both characters are repressed, formal, hemmed in by ideas of politeness and 'the right thing to do'. Both are somewhat awkward in a hotel environment. Really, they would be a perfect match – if it wasn't for the sex thing.

The **mid-point** comes when they actually get into bed together and the sex proves awkward. There is no going back now for either of them.

The **crisis** comes when Edward ejaculates prematurely and Florence, horrified, runs away to Chesil Beach, leaving him humiliated.

The **climax** is the final showdown between Edward and Florence on the beach, where they decide to part for good. Or, rather, Edward refuses to call after her when she walks away – the idea being that you can change a whole life simply by doing nothing.

This is demonstrated in the final part, the **resolution**, where we discover what became of both of them in later life. We learn that if he had called out to her, she would have come back. As it is, Edward is condemned to a life unfulfilled by love.

The story is complex, despite its simplicity, because its themes are multiple. But the principles of structure and character are largely adhered to.

## *The Wonderful Wizard of Oz*

### L. FRANK BAUM (1900; 189 PP.)

As it is a fairy tale, a mythic form of storytelling rather than a classical drama, *Oz* fits more closely the mythic template than the classical one – but, as usual, they overlap.

The book is really quite different from the much more famous film. And certainly, unlike the cinematic version, it doesn't waste any time getting going – in the film the **inciting incident** is preceded by a lengthy sequence about life in Kansas, all filmed in black and white, before the action shifts to the Technicolor world of Oz.

We know little of Dorothy's character in the book except that she is an orphan – always a popular trait for a heroine. The world she lives in is grey and depressing, and so are the people. Her only source of joy is her dog, Toto. Other than this, she is an entirely generic 'little girl'.

Unlike in the movie, Dorothy and her house are sucked up by a tornado almost immediately – on page 5. Thus the *call to adventure* and *crossing the threshold* (and the **inciting incident**) are combined into one supernatural event. (Unless you want to see Dorothy's heading off to the Emerald City to find the Wizard as her *call to adventure*. It's very much a matter of interpretation – in any story, one can play with the names of these turning points loosely. The point is to recognise that they exist and that they matter.)

Dorothy lands in Oz and learns that she has killed the Wicked Witch of the East by doing so. She is told this by someone quickly established as her *mentor* – Glinda, the Good Witch of the South. Dorothy then learns that there were four witches in Oz, two good and two bad, and she has just killed one of the bad ones, to the relief of Glinda and all the Munchkins who live in Oz. There is also one wizard – the Wizard of Oz, who lives in the Emerald City. Dorothy is warned against the Wicked Witch of the West, who will be her antagonist and *enemy*.

Dorothy announces her desire almost as soon as she lands in Oz: to get home again. This is the chief *quest*, the overarching goal or superobjective of the story. Glinda tells her that the only way for her to get home is to go and ask the Wizard, but that is a long journey, sometimes dark and terrible. Classically, the *mentor*, Glinda, cannot go with her (just as, for instance, the Fellowship of the Ring is left to handle its trials alone when Gandalf, in the first part of *The Lord of the Rings*, falls into an abyss, or Luke is left on his own when Ben Kenobi dies fighting Darth Vader in the first *Star Wars* movie).

So – Act Two begins, almost immediately, on page 16. Dorothy learns that the Emerald City is exactly in the centre of the country, and she heads off on the Yellow Brick Road, where she meets her *allies*: the Scarecrow, the Cowardly Lion and the Tin Woodman. Each of them has a flaw, or wound, he needs to heal. (Dorothy doesn't really have a wound to heal, only a problem to solve.)

They have exciting adventures, but by the mid-point Dorothy's antagonist has not really shown up. (In the film the Wicked Witch features much earlier.) Dorothy arrives with her *allies* at the Emerald City and meets the Wizard more or less halfway through the book. This is a key moment: Dorothy learns that she must kill the Wicked Witch in order to return home. In other words, she ceases being (relatively) passive, and becomes urgently proactive. The jeopardy is increased precipitously.

The Wicked Witch sends various *enemies* to attack her, and the flying monkeys bring her back to her castle. This is Dorothy's **crisis**. She is at her lowest ebb and believes she will never get back to Kansas. The Witch wants to kill her, but cannot because of the magical kiss mark on her forehead (given to her by Glinda). The **climax** comes when, after the Witch steals one of Dorothy's silver shoes (in the film they are ruby slippers), Dorothy becomes angry and throws water on the Witch – and she shrivels to nothing.

We are just over 100 pages in, so there is still a long way to go until the end of the book. The film (rightly in my view) dispensed with the long **resolution**, and Dorothy's vanquishing of the Witch is quickly followed by her return to Kansas. However, the mythic-structure template includes a stage missing from the classical structure – the *road back*. And this occupies the remainder of the novel's narrative, where

Dorothy realises how precious home is and how much she is loved. She doesn't actually say, as in the film, 'There's no place like home,' but that is the lesson she has learned, and her **reversal**. So she just about makes the grade as a **three-dimensional character**.

## *Us*

### DAVID NICHOLLS (2014; 396 PP.)

*Us*, like many novels with extensive backstory or flashbacks, is really two connected stories. Both have the same characters and **protagonists**, but are different narratives set in different time frames. Both, crucially, are constantly moving forward, and both are connected to a central spine: the evolution of the **protagonist**'s relationship with his wife and son.

The book was a big success and this was doubtless partly due to its elegant structure, which accords with all the classic principles. The more unusual elements of it are the extreme shortness of the chapters – just one or two pages, usually – and the reliance on backstory, which takes up almost as much of the book as the main story.

It immediately starts with a bang – the **inciting incident**. We learn that the wife, Connie, is leaving the narrator/**protagonist** Douglas. We learn that they had a child who died, and also that they are going on a journey across Europe with their only son, Albie, a teenager with whom Douglas does not get along. The desire/*quest* – for Douglas to win his wife back – is immediately stated. Thus, in the first few pages, we have introduced all the main characters, and established both a *quest* (to get the wife back) and a physical journey (across Europe), as well as a mystery: what happened to the child who died?

The **second act** begins with the commencement of the trip across Europe, a journey that will include visits to the locations of many of the Continent's major artistic treasures. (One of the secondary appeals of the book is that it is a guided tour of European art. Connie is, or was, an artist, who, before she met Douglas, had an important relationship with a romantic, passionate fellow artist, Angelo.)

Connie and Douglas, though happily married for twenty-seven years, are opposites: he is a scientist, reliable, a bit dull, a bit philistine, but a good husband and father; she is clever, artistic, intuitive, a mother who has an excellent relationship with the son that Douglas struggles to get along with.

Douglas starts the trip full of hope (the **dream stage**), but it very quickly descends into the **frustration stage**, as he clearly irritates both his wife and son with his control-freakery. At the **mid-point**, Douglas unintentionally humiliates his son, and Albie simply abandons the trip to go off on his own.

Connie, furious with Douglas and worried for Albie, decides to go home. But Douglas refuses to go with her and sets off to find his son and make amends. Now his jeopardy has deepened – he stands to lose not only his wife, but also his son. So his new *quest* – you might call it a *sub-quest* – is to reconcile with Albie and hope that, if he succeeds, Connie will take him back. This is the **mirror moment**, when he sees himself as he really is. There is even a literal **mirror moment**, when he sees his own reflection and remarks that he is 'unfamiliar' to himself. He is deep in the *void*, or in the heart of the woods, where he must change – or lose everything.

The rest of the narrative concerns his increasingly desperate attempts, travelling across Europe, to find Albie. On the way he meets a Swedish lone traveller, Freya, whom he forms a platonic friendship with.

The **crisis** comes, very clearly, around 300 pages in, when Douglas – dirty, cold, penniless and in jail – comes to believe that he has lost both his wife and his son. This is the culmination of the **nightmare stage**. But after being released from jail, he experiences a change in himself. Instead of being constantly self-effacing and apologetic in the face of strangers, when the commuters he experiences on a train journey regard him with 'wariness', he 'return[s] their stares. What did I care? Like some newly freed jailbird, I was out and back on the streets.'

On the way to Madrid, where he is making a final attempt to locate Albie, he 'peered out of the window like a child – everything was sharp and clear.' His **rebirth** is under way. When he arrives in Madrid for a final attempt to hook up with Albie, he is the opposite of the map-and-schedule-obsessed traveller he started the book as: 'I arrived with no guidebook, no maps, no expectations.'

In the **climax**, he meets with Albie and attempts to apologise, but finally the truth about Albie's sullenness is revealed:

'It's like I'm not even your favourite child,' he complains to Douglas, who realises that he has idealised their lost daughter over Albie – at least in Albie's mind.

They are finally reconciled, and go and visit art galleries together. Albie, instead of being ashamed of Douglas, introduces him to friends as 'my dad the famous scientist'. They get drunk together and even go swimming.

But the story is not quite over yet, for there is a second **climax** – or, if you prefer, **climatic moment**, since, formally speaking, the **climax** constitutes the whole of the third act – when Douglas, stung by a jellyfish, has a heart attack. Now it is Albie who has to look after his father, instead of the opposite, which he does tenderly. A perfect **reversal**. Connie arrives, and she and Douglas have sex.

If this was a Victorian novel, the book would probably end there, with everyone reconciled. But for a more realistic modern readership, Connie subsequently goes back to her old boyfriend, Angelo. But it's OK – Douglas accepts it, and he becomes good friends with both his ex-wife and his son. And, on a final optimistic note, he writes a letter to Freya in the hope that he might start life again... with her.

## *Pride and Prejudice*

### JANE AUSTEN (1813; 325 PP.)

Jane Austen does not waste time in getting the **inciting incident** into the text. It happens on the very first page, when it is announced that a rich, marriageable young man, Bingley, is moving into the nearby Netherfield estate. Mrs Bennet, matriarch of the Bennet family, is delighted, since she is determined to ensure that all her five daughters are married off.

*Pride and Prejudice* comprises a number of different stories and narratives – subplots, if you will: Bingley's on–off courting of Jane; Lizzy's initial romantic interest in Wickham; the absurd Mr Collins's courting of and subsequent rejection by Lizzy, then his taking up with and marrying Lizzy's best friend, Charlotte Lucas. Then, later in the story, Lydia's rash elopement with Wickham.

But there is no doubt about the central story: the love affair between Darcy and Lizzy. This is slow to get launched – Darcy is quite quickly (secretly) smitten by Lizzy but Lizzy is apparently uninterested, even repulsed by Darcy. Why? Because she is prejudiced – in its original meaning. That is, she has prejudged him. That's her flaw. For the first 120 pages we actually hear little about the friction and attraction between these famous lovers.

If there is a **protagonist**, it is Lizzy, but the central desire, which governs the story, is not hers (at least initially), but her mother's passionate wish to see her daughters married. Lizzy's key plot moment comes at the **mid-point**, where, exactly halfway through the book, Mr Darcy, to her astonishment (and apparent horror) proposes to her.

It is the first moment in the book in which Lizzy, who has hitherto been constrained by her impeccable manners (and those of her society), throws off her courtesies and is straightforwardly rude to Darcy. Darcy, who makes a point of his liking for plain speaking, gets plain speaking from Lizzy – right in the neck. It's a classic **reversal**.

This moment changes everything. It propels Darcy into writing the letter that explains to Lizzy that it is Wickham who has dealt unjustly with him, not the other way around. At this point, Lizzy has to begin to acknowledge her prejudice (her inner antagonist), while her external antagonist, Darcy, has to moderate his pride (his own inner antagonist).

It is a collision of opposites. All that follows between them is a consequence of this moment, as Lizzy gradually begins to fall for Darcy and also starts to believe that she has lost him for ever. The **frustration stage** is well under way and the **nightmare stage** is about to begin. (Perhaps the **dream stage** was when Lizzy didn't have to care about Darcy one way or another...)

The **crisis/worst point** comes after Lizzy has given up all hope of Darcy still being interested in her, at the same time as Lydia is running away with the dastardly Wickham, leading to the unbearable suffering of their beloved father.

Darcy comes to the rescue, but Lizzy still believes she has lost him. When Bingley returns to Netherfield, bringing Darcy with him, Lizzy is so embarrassed she hopes never to see him again. But in the **climax**, the lovers are reunited, and in classic romantic novels that only means one thing for the **resolution**: marriage and happy-ever-afters, not only for Lizzy but for Jane, who is finally united with her beloved

Bingley. Finally, the desire that has driven the narrative – Mrs Bennet's – is satisfied, at least for three of her five girls, with the irony that one of them has married an outright cad purely for the money. But otherwise, the theme is clear, just as it was for Lizzy's literary successor, Bridget Jones: true love conquers all.

## *A Girl Is a Half-Formed Thing*

### EIMEAR MCBRIDE (2013; 203 PP.)

This is a modernist novel, very much in the distant wake of James Joyce, and is written in a stream-of-consciousness style. I imagine that McBride was not particularly concerned with plot in writing the book, yet the classic markers of a plot are there all the same.

The **protagonist** is the unnamed narrator, the girl. She has a brother with cancer, who is bullied at school. Their mother favours the brother over her.

The **inciting incident**, classically positioned a quarter of the way in, takes place when, as a thirteen-year-old, the girl has sex with her uncle. The uncle then disappears from the story. She then seems to fall prey to sexual obsession, pursuing boys and men for sex. More or less exactly halfway through, at the **mid-point**, the uncle reappears and they start to have sex again.

After that, the book, from a plot point of view, becomes unfocused. Shortly after the **mid-point** the brother's cancer reappears, and the girl intensifies her search for sexual encounters by encouraging violence and risky sex with a variety of boys and men. The uncle turns up again four-fifths of the way through, but she seems to have lost interest in him, although the affair continues, and later she (sort of) gets raped by him. (It's hard to be completely sure – this is a book in which motivations are often obscure.)

Soon after this, her brother dies and then the girl is randomly raped by a complete stranger. This is unequivocally violent, criminal rape, which crushes her, and which you could definitely describe as the **worst point** in a novel pretty much crammed with a plethora of **worst points**.

Shortly after, in the **climax**, she drowns herself. **Resolution** and end of story. There is a kind of **reversal** – in that she undergoes the most fundamental change, from alive to dead. And there is the collision of opposites – innocence (girl) and experience (uncle) – or, if you prefer, innocence and corruption.

It is very hard to apply the standard questions to a text like this. What is the narrator seeking? Oblivion? Probably. What is the meaning of her initial apparent acquiescence in, even welcoming of, her uncle's sexual abuse? Hard to say. What does the end mean? Probably that everything is meaningless and there's no hope – at least for someone with such ill fortune. One can bring one's own meanings. If ever there was a book primarily about character, this is it – but only one character, the girl, who is racked by conflicting desires.

Whatever the case, even McBride, it seems, with all her apparent commitment to shapeless modernism, cannot help but tell some sort of story in the end. Most of the classic plot points are here, and help hold the novel together.

## *The Reader*

### BERNHARD SCHLINK (1995; 216 PP.)

*The Reader* is a beautifully structured (and written) novel, doubtless one of the reasons that, in 2008, it was made into a film (starring Kate Winslet). The narrative never stops moving forward; it never stops developing character; it doesn't waste a word.

The **inciting incident** grabs the reader's attention immediately: a fifteen-year-old schoolboy, Michael, who is unwell and being kept from school, gets involved with a woman, Hanna, a tram conductor twice his age, in post-Second World War Germany. He goes to her flat, they become intimate and we watch their relationship develop. In terms of character, Hanna is mysterious and somewhat distant; Michael is naive and curious.

On one occasion Hanna comes to Michael's home and is fascinated by his father's library. She loves more than anything having Michael read to her. He sees her as fundamentally good: 'whatever there is in a tiger – that evil something – that's not you,' he tells her.

One day she comes to visit him at a public swimming

pool and he does not acknowledge her. The next day, when he visits her flat, she has disappeared. The disappearance marks the end of Act One, and leaves the reader with a question: why did she go? This is never satisfactorily answered, but it provides some fuel for the **second act**.

Act Two begins with a jump forward in time: we find Michael as an adult, trained as a lawyer, attending a war-crimes trial. He describes himself at that time (as he looks back on the events as an older man) as 'arrogant' and 'superior'. He recognises Hanna as one of the defendants in a case in which a group of Jewish villagers were burnt to death in a church, something that Hanna and her colleagues, all concentration-camp guards, did nothing to prevent.

He feels numb when he sees her and does not react emotionally. In a key moment, Michael realises that Hanna cannot read or write, and is actually willing to go to jail to protect her secret, so great is her shame. But her shame is about being illiterate, not the murder of the Jews.

The **mid-point** comes around 100 pages in, when, in a tense scene, Hanna – who is being interrogated by the judge about the incident, and defending herself by saying that she was 'doing her job' – asks the judge 'what would you have done?' And the judge cannot answer.

This, perhaps, is the question at the heart of the book. She comes across not as a villain, but as either terrifyingly honest or utterly naive. This is the mystery of the book – she is an ordinary woman, no monster, who collaborated in a monstrous act. Is that 'evil thing' really in her alone? Or is it also in the judge? And in Michael?

Shortly afterwards, Michael visits the site of a concentration camp, where the taxi driver who takes him half admits that he was also responsible for killing Jews. Michael asks himself: 'Would she [Hanna] have sent me to the gas chamber?' At the end of the trial, Hanna leaves the court looking 'proud, wounded, lost, and infinitely tired'. She is sent to prison. This ends the **second act**.

In the third act, Michael falls ill, just as he was ill at the start of the book. Then his numbness suddenly disappears and he is overcome with feeling. He tries to understand how he could have loved a war criminal. He records himself reading books aloud and sends the tapes to Hanna in prison, but he does not visit her. He does this for ten years. At the heart of the **climax**, he meets Hanna again. She is about to be released and the prison governor asks that Michael find her somewhere to live. But on the day she is meant to leave, Michael receives a message that she has been found hanged in her cell.

In the **resolution**, Michael takes tea with the daughter of one of the survivors of the fire. This scene deals with the damage Hanna did to Michael, and links her to the failure of all his future relationships (Michael is divorced). Hanna has left some money with a note requesting Michael to give it to the daughter of the survivor, but the daughter will not accept it, because she thinks it will grant Hanna, posthumously, a form of absolution. She suggests that Michael give the money to Jewish charities instead. He duly gives the money to a Jewish charity for illiteracy.

*The Reader*, then, has a beginning, a middle and an end. It has three acts. It has a **mid-point**, a **climax** and a **resolution**, and even a **crisis**, if you want to see Hanna's committal to prison as a **worst point**, although that might be simplistic. This helps keep the novel thoroughly readable. But, in the end, the plot is only a skeleton to hang the complex, tortured flesh of the book on. As Milan Kundera remarks:

> A novel does not assert anything; a novel searches and poses questions... The stupidity of people comes from having an answer for everything... The novelist teaches the reader to comprehend the world as a question.

## *The Prime of Miss Jean Brodie*
### MURIEL SPARK (1961; 128 PP.)

If ever there was a novel that could be described as 'character-driven' it is *The Prime of Miss Jean Brodie*. Although it is not a modernist novel, it flips about constantly from character to character and back and forth in time. Much of it is about the relationship between the eponymous Jean Brodie and six schoolgirls – Sandy, Jenny, Rose, Mary, Monica and Eunice – at the Marcia Blaine School in Edinburgh in the 1930s, but a fair amount of this very short novel takes place long after the girls have left school and grown into adults.

The central narrative shows the girls' development between the ages of eleven and eighteen. The structure that is contained in the novel is sliced up and sprinkled about the text. Information that would normally be withheld for tension leaks out all the time, so the real charm of the book is to find out 'How did that happen?' rather than experiencing the surprise of it actually happening.

*The Prime of Miss Jean Brodie* doesn't even have one particular **protagonist** (although it clearly has a central character – Jean Brodie herself). And the stories of many characters are all simultaneously juggled, so to talk of a single **climax** or **mid-point** is difficult.

A structure, though, is nevertheless discernible.

Brodie herself is resolutely two-dimensional, but fascinating all the same. The action is governed by Jean Brodie's desire to hold on to and influence the six girls who make up the 'Brodie set', favoured by her for special attention and privilege. There is a mystery of sorts, since we learn relatively early on that Brodie was eventually betrayed by one of her girls and as a result lost her job. But we are not sure which one. Throughout the story, Brodie is in a sort of jeopardy (even though we know the outcome), since the headmistress, Miss Mackay, wants to get rid of both her and the Brodie set. Thus, Brodie has an antagonist from the start. But the book is essentially a series of vignettes, carefully arranged to constitute a story.

To the extent that there is a plot, it focuses on the question (posed by, and seen through the eyes of, the schoolgirls) of whether Brodie had an affair with Gordon Lowther, the music teacher, or Teddy Lloyd, the one-armed art teacher, who is married. It turns out it was Lowther. And we learn that it was her favourite, Sandy, who committed the betrayal that led to her dismissal. These central facts we learn at the **mid-point**. The knowledge that she was betrayed in the first place comes early, on page 27. (Whether this can be seen as an **inciting incident** is a moot point in such a variously structured piece of work.)

Sandy and Jenny, the central schoolgirl characters, fantasise and make up stories about Brodie and her lovers in which they place themselves as characters. After the girls move to senior school, Teddy Lloyd starts painting them. The paintings, tellingly, all look like Jean Brodie. Teddy and Sandy start an affair. But the real love affair in the book is between Brodie and her girls. And by the end we have seen that it is an abusive relationship – Brodie simply wants to live out her bourgeois, disappointing life through the medium of her 'set'.

Then they are sixteen. By this time pressures on Brodie are increasing from school authorities. And we hear to Brodie's surprise that Mr Lowther is marrying Miss Lockhart, the science teacher. Now Brodie plots to have Rose as Teddy Lloyd's lover – as a kind of avatar for herself.

When the girls are seventeen, a rich, delinquent girl, Joyce Emily, appears in the narrative. Her brother went to fight in the Spanish Civil War. (By now we are in 1937.) Brodie takes her up as a new 'Brodie girl'. She runs away to Spain and is killed. Sandy realises that Brodie is entirely serious in setting up Rose as Teddy Lloyd's lover. She is taken aback by the perversity of the idea that Rose should become his lover in Jean Brodie's stead (since Brodie sees herself as having heroically forgone her true love, Teddy, because he is married).

Brodie travels to Germany and Austria in 1938 and has become a fan of Hitler. Very close to the end of the book, we learn that it is Brodie who urged Joyce Emily to go to Spain and fight for General Franco in the Spanish Civil War. Then we hear that Miss Mackay is still after Brodie and that the latter has formed a new set of 'Brodie girls'. Sandy has decided she wants to put a stop to Miss Brodie. The **climax** comes right at the end, when Miss Mackay finally manages to find a reason to sack Jean Brodie – not for her liberal views on sex, but for the fact that she encouraged Joyce Emily to support Franco. By this time we learn from Miss Mackay that Brodie is past her 'prime' and 'likes her wee drink'.

After being forced out of the school, Miss Brodie becomes obsessed with finding out who betrayed her. But she never does.

This is a book that focuses on theme and character – the theme being how people in positions of power can damage those in their trust. Or perhaps it's about the dangers of romanticism. Or perhaps it's about betrayal. You can form your own conclusions. But if the narrative characters can be likened to an orchestra playing a tune (theme), then Jean Brodie is the lead musician. And it is her carelessness and corruption that are at the heart of the music.

# APPENDIX 4

## *Want and Need at the Mid-point*

Halfway through *King Lear*, naked on the blasted heath, Lear discovers that what he *wants* – to maintain his kingly power – is not what he *needs*.

What he *needs* is to incorporate Cordelia's honesty, humility and compassion into his own hitherto overbearing, bullying character.

Bridget Jones begins to discover that what she *wants* – to make the charismatic Daniel Cleaver her boyfriend – is not what she *needs*. She realises this after, at the mid-point, Cleaver breaks her heart by revealing he is engaged to be married to someone else.

At the mid-point of *Pride and Prejudice*, Lizzy discovers she has misjudged Mr Darcy. And now she begins to register her true feelings for him, and how much she has been prejudiced against him. That's her flaw. While Darcy has to begin abandoning his pride. That's his.

In the middle of the film *The Queen*, Elizabeth II – as she witnesses an injured stag, which later dies – discovers that what she *wants* (to hold on strictly to her traditional role as a distant and dispassionate monarch) is not what she *needs*.

What she *needs* is compassion and sensitivity to the feelings of others.

In *Great Expectations*, Pip, in his rejection of his beloved stepfather Joe Gargery, begins his journey of learning that what he *wants* – to be a gentleman and win Estella – is not what he *needs*, which is to learn humility.

# BIBLIOGRAPHY

Aristotle, *Poetics*

Christopher Booker, *The Seven Basic Plots: Why We Tell Stories* (2004)

Robert Olen Butler, *From Where You Dream: The Process of Writing Fiction* (2006)

Joseph Campbell, *The Hero with a Thousand Faces* (1949)

David Corbett, *The Art of Character: Creating Memorable Characters for Fiction, Film, and TV* (2013)

Lisa Cron, *Story Genius: How to Use Brain Science to Go Beyond Outlining and Write a Riveting Novel* (2016)

E. M. Forster, *Aspects of the Novel* (1927)

Patricia Highsmith, *Plotting and Writing Suspense Fiction* (1966)

Robert McKee, *Story: Substance, Structure, Style, and the Principles of Screenwriting* (1997)

David Mamet, *Three Uses of the Knife: On the Nature and Purpose of Drama* (1998)

George Saunders, *A Swim in a Pond in the Rain* (2021)

Richard Skinner, *Fiction Writing: The Essential Guide to Writing a Novel* (2009)

Will Storr, *The Science of Storytelling: Why Stories Make Us Human, and How to Tell Them Better* (2019)
Christopher Vogler, *The Writer's Journey: Mythic Structure for Writers* (2007)
Nigel Watts, *Write a Novel: And Get It Published* (2010)
James Wood, *How Fiction Works* (2008)
John Yorke, *Into the Woods: How Stories Work and Why We Tell Them* (2013)

# ACKNOWLEDGEMENTS

My thanks to my brilliant friend and agent Ruth Cairns, without whom I can definitely state that this book would not have happened. Thank you so much for your faith and encouragement. Also to Mark Richards and everyone at Swift Press, who helped produce this book with such professionalism and commitment.